THE PICNIC
and Suchlike Pandemonium

GERALD DURRELL

THE PICNIC
and Suchlike Pandemonium

COLLINS
St James's Place, London
1979

William Collins Sons & Co Ltd
London · Glasgow · Sydney · Auckland
Toronto · Johannesburg

First published 1979
© Gerald Durrell 1979

ISBN 0 00 216731 X

Set in Imprint
Made and printed in Great Britain by
William Collins Sons & Co Ltd, Glasgow

CONTENTS

This book is for my sister Margo,
who has let me lampoon her in print,
with great good humour.
With love.

THE PICNIC

———————————◆———————————

The months of March and April of that year had been unprecedentedly dry and warm for England. The farmers, caught by surprise by the novelty of a situation which did not allow them to plead bankruptcy because of unusually late frost, rallied gamely and started talking about the horrors of drought. People who had, the previous autumn, informed us that the wonderful crop of berries and mushrooms were signs of a hard winter and an even harder summer to follow, now said that a surfeit of berries and mushrooms meant a fine spring the following year. To top it all, those paid Munchausens amongst us, the weather forecasters, predicted an extremely hot spell from April to August. The English, being gullible, got so overexcited at these predictions that many of them went to extreme lengths, like laying in suntan oil and deck chairs. In the whole length and breadth of Bournemouth, on the south coast, where we were living, there was not a pair of bathing trunks nor a sunshade to be had for love or money.

My family, all sun-worshippers, responded like buds to the warmth. They quarrelled more, they sang more, they argued more, they drank and ate more, because outside in the garden the spring flowers were in riotous sweet-scented bloom and the sun, though only butter-yellow, had real heat in it. But of all the family, it was my mother who was moved to a strange fervour by the meteorological forecasts that were being mooted about, principally, I think, because she heard these predictions from the radio.

To Mother, this made all the difference; the difference between reading your horoscope in a women's magazine and having your future told by a genuine gypsy on the steps of his caravan. Throughout the war, the British government, including Churchill (when he was not otherwise engaged) lived inside our radio set for the express purpose of keeping Mother informed as to the progress of the war, and the imminence of the German invasion. They had never told her a lie and, more important, they had won the war. Now, of course, the war was over, but the integrity of the men who had lived in the radio was just as impeccable as it had been of yore. When she heard farmers talking of thousands of cattle dying of thirst or reservoirs drying up, anonymous doctors giving tips on how to avoid sun-stroke, and of beauty consultants advising on how to get a tan without withering away, Mother naturally concluded that we were in for a heat-wave that would make the West Indies seem like an extension of Alaska.

'I've thought of a wonderful way of welcoming Larry back,' she said one morning at breakfast.

Larry, who of his own volition had been absent from England for some ten years, was paying a flying visit in order to attend to the promotion of one of his books. In spite of a letter from him saying how the thought of returning to what he called Pudding Island revolted him, Mother was convinced that he was pining for the sights and sounds of 'Merry England' after so many years as an exile.

'Who wants to welcome him?' asked Leslie, helping himself liberally to marmalade.

'Leslie, dear, you know you don't mean that,' said Mother. 'It will be so nice to have the family all together again after so long.'

'Larry always causes trouble,' said my sister Margo. 'He's so critical.'

'I wouldn't say he was critical,' said Mother, untruthfully. 'He just sees things a little differently.'

'You mean he wants everyone to agree with him,' said Leslie.

'Yes,' said Margo, 'that's right. He always thinks he knows best.'

'He's entitled to his opinion, dear,' said Mother. 'That's what we fought the war for.'

'What? So that we'd all have to agree with Larry's opinion?' asked Leslie.

'You know perfectly well what I mean, Leslie,' replied Mother, sternly. 'So don't try and muddle me up.'

'What's your idea?' asked Margo.

'Well,' began Mother, 'it's going to be unbearably hot . . .'

'Who says so?' interrupted Leslie, disbelievingly.

'The wireless,' said Mother, crushingly, as though speaking of the Delphic oracle. 'The wireless says we are in for an unprecedented trough of high pressure.'

'I'll believe it when I see it,' said Leslie gloomily.

'But it was on the wireless, dear,' explained Mother. 'It's not just a rumour – it came from the Air Ministry roof.'

'Well, I don't trust the Air Ministry, either,' said Leslie.

'Neither do I,' agreed Margo. 'Not since they let George Matchman become a pilot.'

'They didn't?' said Leslie incredulously. 'He's as blind as a bat, *and* he drinks like a fish.'

'And he's got B.O., too,' put in Margo, damningly.

'I really don't see what George Matchman's got to do with the weather on the Air Ministry roof,' protested Mother, who had never got used to the number of hares her family could start from a normal conversation.

'It's probably George up there on the roof,' said Leslie.

'And I wouldn't trust *him* to tell me the time.'

'It's not George,' said Mother firmly. 'I know his voice.'

'Anyway, what's your idea?' asked Margo again.

'Well,' continued Mother, 'as the Air Ministry roof says we are going to have fine weather, I think we ought to take Larry out to see the English countryside at its best. He must have been missing it. I know when your father and I used to come home from India, we always liked a spin in the country. I suggest we ask Jack to take us out for a picnic in the Rolls.'

There was a moment's silence while the family digested the idea.

'Larry won't agree,' said Leslie at last. 'You know what he's like. If he doesn't like it, he'll carry on terribly: you know him.'

'I'm sure he'll be very pleased,' said Mother, but without total conviction. The vision of my elder brother 'carrying on' had flashed across her mind.

'I know, let's surprise him,' suggested Margo. 'We'll put all the food and stuff in the boot and just say we're going for a short drive.'

'Where would we go?' asked Leslie.

'Lulworth Cove,' said Mother.

'That's not a short drive,' complained Leslie.

'But if he doesn't see the food, he won't suspect,' said Margo triumphantly.

'After he's been driving for an hour and a half, he'll begin to,' Leslie pointed out. 'Even Larry.'

'No, I think we'll just have to tell him it's a sort of a welcome home present,' said Mother. 'After all, we haven't seen him for ten years.'

'Ten peaceful years,' corrected Leslie.

'They weren't at all peaceful,' said Mother. 'We had the war.'

'I meant peaceful without Larry,' explained Leslie.

'Leslie, dear, you shouldn't say things like that, even as a joke,' said Mother reprovingly.

'I'm not joking,' said Leslie.

'He can't make a fuss if it's a welcome home picnic,' put in Margo.

'Larry can make a fuss about everything,' replied Leslie with conviction.

'Don't exaggerate,' said Mother. 'We'll ask Jack about the Rolls when he comes in. What's he doing?'

'Dismantling it, I expect,' said Leslie.

'Oh, he does annoy me!' complained Margo. 'We've had that damn car for three months and it's spent more time dismantled than mantled. He makes me sick. Every time I want to go out in it, he's got the engine all over the garage.'

'You shouldn't have married an engineer,' said Leslie. 'You know what they're like; they have to take everything to pieces. Compulsive wreckers.'

'Well, we'll ask him to make a special effort and have the Rolls all in one piece for Larry,' concluded Mother. 'I'm sure he'll agree.'

The Rolls in question was a magnificent 1922 model that Jack had discovered lurking shame-facedly in some remote country garage, her paint unwashed, her chrome unkempt, but still a lady of high degree. He had purchased her for the princely sum of two hundred pounds, and brought her back to the house in triumph, where, under his tender ministrations, she had blossomed, and was christened Esmerelda. Her coach-work now dazzled the eye, her walnut fittings glowed with polish, her engine was undefiled by so much as a speck of oil; she had running boards, a soft top you could put back for fine weather, a glass panel which could be wound up so that the driver could not hear your strictures on the working classes, and – best of all – a strange, trumpet-like telephone thing through which you shouted instructions to the chauffeur. It was as wonderful as owning a dinosaur. Both the back and front seats would accommodate four people with room to spare. There was a built-in walnut cabinet for drinks, and a boot that appeared big enough to contain four cabin trunks or twelve suitcases. No expense could be spared on such a vehicle, and so, by some underground method, Jack had produced a continental fire-engine horn which let out an ear-splitting, arrogant ta-*ta*, ta-*ta*. This was only pressed into service in extreme emergencies; normally, the huge, black, rubber bulb horn was employed, which made a noise like a deferential Californian sea-lion. This was suitable for hurrying up old ladies on pedestrian crossings, but the fire-engine horn could make a double-decker bus cringe into the ditch to let us pass.

Just at that moment Jack, in his shirt-sleeves and liberally besmeared with oil, came in to breakfast. He was a man of medium height with a mop of curly dark hair, prominent bright blue eyes, and a nose any Roman emperor would have been glad to possess. It was a nose that really *was* a nose; a nose to be reckoned with; a nose of size and substance, one that would have warmed the cockles of Cyrano de Bergerac's heart, a nose that heralded the cold weather, the opening of the pubs, mirth, or any other important event, with a flamboyant colour change that a chameleon would have envied. It was a nose to be arrogant with, or to shelter behind in moments of stress. It was a nose which could be proud or comic, according to the mood; a nose that once seen was never forgotten, like the beak of a duck-billed platypus.

'Ah!' said Jack, and his nose quivered and took on a rubicund sheen. 'Do I smell kippers?'

'There, in the kitchen, keeping warm,' said Mother.

'Where have you been?' asked Margo, unnecessarily, since Jack's oil-covered condition stated clearly where he had been.

'Cleaning Esmerelda's engine,' replied Jack, equally unnecessarily.

He went out into the kitchen and returned with two kippers lying on a plate. He sat down, and started to dissect them.

'I don't know what you find to do with that car,' said Margo. 'You're always taking it to pieces.'

'I knew a man once who had a wonderful way with kippers,' remarked Jack to me, oblivious of my sister's complaints. 'He'd sort of turn them on their backs and somehow get all the bones out in one go. Very clever. They all came out, just like that. Like harp strings, you know . . . I still can't quite see how he did it.'

'What's wrong with it?' asked Margo.

'What's wrong with what?' countered her husband vaguely, staring at his kippers as if he could hypnotize the bones out of them.

'The Rolls,' said Margo.

'Esmerelda?' asked Jack in alarm. 'What's wrong with her?'

'That's what I'm asking *you*,' said Margo. 'You really are the most irritating man.'

'There's nothing wrong with her,' replied Jack. 'Beautiful piece of work.'

'It would be, if we went out in her occasionally,' pointed out Margo, sarcastically. 'She's not very beautiful sitting in the garage with all her innards out.'

'You can't say innards out,' Jack objected. 'Innards are in, they can't be out.'

'Oh, you do infuriate me!' said Margo.

'Now, now, dear,' said Mother. 'If Jack says there's nothing wrong with the car, then everything's all right.'

'All right for what?' asked Jack, mystified.

'We were thinking of taking Larry out for a picnic when he comes,' Mother explained, 'and we thought it would be nice to do it in the Rolls.'

Jack thought about this, munching on his kippers.

'That's a good idea,' he said at last, to our surprise. 'I've just tuned the engine. It'll do her good to have a run. Where were you thinking of going?'

'Lulworth,' said Mother. 'It's very pretty, the Purbecks.'

'There's some good hills there, too,' said Jack with enthusiasm. 'That'll tell me if her clutch is slipping.'

Fortified with the knowledge that the Rolls would be intact

for the picnic, Mother threw herself with enthusiasm into the task of preparing for it. As usual, the quantity of food she prepared for the day would have been sufficient to victual Napoleon's army during its retreat from Moscow. There were curry-puffs and Cornish pasties, raised ham pies and a large game pie, three roast chickens, two large loaves of home-made bread, a treacle tart, brandy snaps and some meringues; to say nothing of three kinds of home-made chutney and jams, as well as biscuits, a fruit cake, and a sponge. When this was all assembled on the kitchen table, she called us in to have a look.

'Do you think there'll be enough?' she asked, worriedly.

'I thought we were only going to Lulworth for the afternoon?' said Leslie. 'I didn't realize we were emigrating.'

'Mother, it's far too much,' exclaimed Margo. 'We'll never eat it all.'

'Nonsense! Why, in Corfu I used to take twice as much,' said Mother.

'But in Corfu we used to have twelve or fourteen people,' Leslie pointed out. 'There's only six of us, you know.'

'It looks like a two years' supply of food for a Red Cross shipment to a famine area,' said Jack.

'It's not all *that* much,' said Mother, defensively. 'You know how Larry likes his food, and we'll be eating by the sea, and the sea air always gives one an appetite.'

'Well, I hope Esmerelda's boot will hold it all,' commented Jack.

The next afternoon, Mother insisted, in spite of our protests, that we all dress up in our finery to go down to the station to meet Larry. Owing to the inordinately long time Margo took to find the right shade of lipstick, Mother's plans were thwarted, for, just as we were about to enter the Rolls, a taxi drew up. Inside was Larry, having caught an earlier train. He lowered the window of the cab and glared at us.

'Larry, dear!' cried Mother. 'What a lovely surprise!'

Larry made his first verbal communication to his family in ten years.

'Have any of you got colds?' he rasped, irritably. 'If so, I'll go to an hotel.'

'Colds?' said Mother. 'No, dear. Why?'

'Well, everyone else in this God-forsaken island has one,' said Larry, as he climbed out of the cab. 'I've spent a week in London running for my life from a barrage of cold germs. Everyone sneezing and snuffling like a brood of catarrhal bulldogs. You should have heard them on the train – hawking and spitting and coughing like some bloody travelling TB sanitorium. I spent the journey locked up in the lavatory, holding my nose and squirting a nasal spray through the keyhole. How you survive this pestilential island, defeats me. I swear to you that there were so many people with colds in London, it was worse than the Great Plague.'

He paid off the taxi, and walked into the house ahead of us, carrying his suitcase. He was wearing a deer-stalker hat in a dog-tooth tweed, and a suit in a singularly unattractive tartan, the ground colour of which was dog-sick green with a dull red stripe over it. He looked like a diminutive and portly Sherlock Holmes.

'Mercifully, we are cold-free,' said Mother, following him into the house. 'It's this lovely fine weather we've been having. Would you like some tea, dear?'

'I'd rather have a large whisky and soda,' said Larry, taking a half empty bottle out of the capacious pocket of his coat. 'It's better for colds.'

'But you said you hadn't got a cold,' pointed out Mother.

'I haven't,' replied Larry, pouring himself out a large drink. 'This is in case I get one. It's what is called preventive medicine.'

It was obvious that he had been using preventive medicine on the way down, for he grew more and more convivial as the evening drew on; so much so that Mother felt she could broach the subject of the picnic.

'We thought,' she said, 'since the Air Ministry's roof is emphatic about the terribly hot weather, that we might take the Rolls out and go for a picnic tomorrow.'

'Don't you think that's a bit churlish, going off and leaving me after a ten-year exile?' asked Larry.

'Don't be silly, dear,' said Mother. 'You come too.'

'Not a picnic in England,' protested Larry, brokenly. 'I don't think I'm up to it. How I remember it from my youth! All the thrill of ants and sand in the food, trying to light a fire with damp wood, the howling gales, the light snowfall, just as you're munching your first cucumber sandwich . . .'

'No, no, dear. The Air Ministry roof says we're having an unprecedented ridge of high pressure,' said Mother. 'To-morrow's going to be very hot, it said.'

'It may be hot on the Air Ministry roof, but is it going to be hot down here?' enquired Larry.

'Of course,' insisted Mother stoutly.

'Well, I'll think about it,' promised Larry as, carrying the remains of the whisky in case germs attacked him in the night, he made his way to bed.

Next morning dawned blue and breathless, the sun already warm at seven o'clock. Everything augured well. Mother, in order to leave no stone unturned in her efforts to keep Larry in a good mood, gave him his breakfast in bed. Even Margo, in the interests of peace, refrained from giving us our normal excruciating half-hour when she sang the latest pop tunes in the bath, without the benefit of knowing either the tune or the lyric with any degree of certainty.

By ten o'clock, the Rolls had been loaded up and we were preparing to go. Jack made some last-minute slight but important adjustment to the engine, Mother counted the food packages for the last time, and Margo had to go back into the house three times to get various items that she had forgotten. At last we were ready and assembled on the pavement.

'Don't you think we ought to have the roof down, since it's such a nice day?' suggested Jack.

'Oh, yes, dear,' said Mother. 'Let's take advantage of the weather while we've got it.'

Between them Leslie and Jack lowered the canvas roof of the Rolls. We entered the car, and were soon bowling along through the English countryside, as lush and as green and as miniature as you could wish for, full of birdsong. Even pieces of woodland on the rolling Purbeck hills were set in bas-relief against the blue sky in which, high and faint, like the ghosts of minnows, a few threads of cloud hung immobile. The air was fragrant, the sun was warm and the car, purring softly as a sleepy bumble-bee, slid smoothly between tall hedges, breasted green hills, and swept like a hawk down into valleys where the cottages clustered under their thatched roofs so that each village looked as though it was in need of a haircut.

'Yes,' commented Larry, musingly, 'I'd forgotten how Victorian dolls' house the English landscape could look.'

'Isn't it lovely, dear?' said Mother. 'I knew you'd like it.'

We had just swept through a hamlet of white-washed cottages, each with a thatch that looked like an out-sized pie-crust on top, when Jack suddenly stiffened behind the wheel.

'There!' he barked suddenly. 'Didn't you hear it? Distinctly. Tickety-tickety-ping, and then a sort of scroobling noise.'

There was a pause.

'I would have thought,' Larry observed to Mother, 'that this family was quite unbalanced enough without adding insanity by marriage.'

'There it goes again. The scrooble! The scrooble! Can't you hear it?' cried Jack, his eyes gleaming fanatically.

'Oh, God!' said Margo bitterly. 'Why is it we can't go any-where without you wanting to take the car to pieces?'

'But it might be serious,' said Jack. 'That tickety-tickety-ping might be a cracked magneto head.'

'I think it was just a stone you kicked up,' said Leslie.

'No, no,' said Jack. 'That's quite a different ping. That's just a ping without the tickety.'

'Well, I didn't hear any tickety,' said Leslie.

'Nobody ever hears his tickety except him,' complained Margo, angrily. 'It makes me sick!'

'Now, now, dear – don't quarrel,' said Mother, peaceably. 'After all, Jack is the engineer of the family.'

'If he's an engineer, it's a curious sort of technical language they are teaching them now,' commented Larry. 'Engineers in my day never discussed their tickety-pings in public.'

'If you think it's serious, Jack,' said Mother, 'we'd better stop and let you have a look at it.'

So Jack pulled into a lay-by, flanked with willows in bloom, leapt out of the car, opened the bonnet, and flung himself into the bowels of Esmerelda, as a man dying of thirst would throw himself into a desert pool. There were a few loud groans and some grunts, and then a high nasal humming noise that sounded like an infuriated wasp caught in a zither. It was our brother-in-law humming.

'Well,' said Larry, 'since it seems that our postillion has been struck by lightning, how about a life-giving drink?'

'Isn't it a bit early, dear?' asked Mother.

'It may be too early for the English,' observed Larry, 'but don't forget that I've been living among a lot of loose-moraled foreigners who don't think that there's one special time for pleasure, and who don't feel that you're putting your immortal soul in danger every time you have a drink, day *or* night.'

'Very well, dear,' said Mother. 'Perhaps a small drink would be nice.'

Leslie broached the boot and passed us out the drinks.

'If we *had* to stop, this is quite a pleasant spot,' said Larry, condescendingly, gazing round at the rolling green hills, chessboarded by tall hedges, and patterned here and there with the black and frothy green of woodland.

'And the sun really is remarkably hot,' put in Mother. 'It's quite extraordinary for the time of year.'

'We shall pay for it in winter, I suppose,' said Leslie, gloomily. 'We always seem to.'

Just at that moment, from beneath the bonnet of the car, came a loud reverberating sneeze. Larry froze, his glass half-way to his mouth.

'What was that?' he asked.

'Jack,' answered Leslie.

'That noise?' exclaimed Larry. 'That was Jack?'

'Yes,' said Leslie. 'Jack sneezing.'

'Dear God!' cried Larry. 'He's brought a bloody germ with him. Mother, I've spent a week avoiding infection by every means known to the British Medical Association, only to be transported out here into the wilderness without a medical practitioner within fifty miles, to be bombarded by cold germs by my own brother-in-law. It really is too much!'

'Now, now, dear,' said Mother soothingly. 'People sneeze without having colds, you know.'

'Not in England,' said Larry. 'The sneeze in England is the harbinger of misery, even death. I sometimes think the only pleasure an Englishman has is in passing on his cold germs.'

'Larry, dear, you do exaggerate,' said Mother. 'Jack only sneezed once.'

Jack sneezed again.

'There you are!' said Larry, excitedly. 'That's the second time. I tell you, he's working up for an epidemic. Why don't we leave him here; he can easily hitch a lift back into Bourne-mouth, and Leslie can drive.'

'You can't just leave him on the roadside, Larry, don't be silly,' said Mother.

'Why not?' asked Larry. 'The Eskimos put their old people out on ice-floes to be eaten by polar bears.'

'I don't see why Jack has to be eaten by a polar bear just because you're frightened of a stupid little cold,' exclaimed Margo, indignantly.

'I was speaking figuratively,' said Larry. 'In this area, he'd probably be pecked to death by cuckoos.'

'Well, I'm not having him left, anyway,' said Margo.

At that moment, Jack emerged from under the bonnet of the car. His ample nose seemed to have grown to twice its normal size, and to have assumed the colouring of an over-ripe persimmon. His eyes were half closed and watering copiously. He approached the car, sneezing violently.

'Go away!' shouted Larry. 'Take your filthy germs into the fields!'

'Id's nod germs,' said Jack, endeavouring to enunciate with clarity. 'Id's by hay feber.'

'I don't want to know the scientific name for it – just take it away!' shouted Larry. 'Who the hell do you think I am? Louis Pasteur? Bringing your bloody germs to me.'

'Id's hay feber,' Jack repeated, sneezing violently. 'Dere must be some damn flower or udder growing here.' He glanced about balefully through streaming eyes and spotted the willows. 'Ah!' he snarled, through a flurry of sneezes, 'dad's id, der bloody things.'

'I can't understand a word he's saying,' said Larry. 'This cold's unhinged what passed for his mind.'

'It's his hay fever,' explained Margo. 'The willows have started it up.'

'But that's *worse* than a cold,' said Larry in alarm. 'I don't want to catch hay fever.'

'You can't catch it, dear,' said Mother. 'It's an allergy.'

'I don't care if it's an anagram,' said Larry. 'I'm not having it breathed all over *me*.'

'But it's not infectious,' insisted Margo.

'Are you sure?' asked Larry. 'There's always a first time. I expect the first leper said that to his wife, and before she knew what was happening, she'd founded a colony, all ringing their bells and shouting "unclean".'

'You do complicate things, dear,' said Mother. 'It's perfectly ordinary hay fever.'

'We muzt ged away from deze trees,' said Jack. He entered
the car and drove us off at such a furious pace that we just
missed hitting a large wagon of manure pulled by two giant
Shire horses, which was coming round the corner.

'I don't remember entering into any suicide pact with him,'
cried Larry, clinging to the door.

'Not so fast,' said Margo. 'You're going too fast.'

'Air!' groaned Jack. 'God to have air to ged rid of de pollen.'

After a few miles of furious driving, accompanied by squeaks
of alarm from Mother and Margo and admonitory roars from
Larry, Jack had taken sufficient air through his nose to ease his
affliction somewhat. We settled down to a more sedate pace.

'I should never have set foot in England again. I knew it,'
complained Larry. 'First it's cold germs, then it's hay fever,
then a death-defying ride like something out of Ben Hur.
When you get to my age, you can't stand this sort of pace without getting a coronary.'

Just before lunchtime, we discovered that we were en-
meshed in the maze of little lanes that led all over the head-
lands and the cliffs. In our efforts to try to find Lulworth Cove,
we got ourselves thoroughly lost, but at last we followed a road
that led down to a circular bay guarded by tall cliffs. The bay
looked blue and serene in the sunshine, so we decided to stop
and have lunch there. Apart from an elderly couple exercising
their dog, the beach was deserted.

'How fortunate,' said Mother. 'We've got the beach to ourselves. I was afraid this fine weather might bring out a lot of
people.'

'Let's walk half-way round the bay,' suggested Leslie. 'It's
not very far, and you get a better view.'

Having all agreed to this plan, we parked the Rolls and, stag-
gering under the burden of food and drink and rugs to sit on,
made our way across the shingle.

'I must have something to sit against,' said Mother. 'Otherwise I get terrible back-ache.'

'Yes, you must recline in a civilized manner,' agreed Larry, 'otherwise you'll get your viscera in a knot. It leads to ulcers and all sorts of things. Your guts rot and your food falls through into the stomach cavity.'

'Larry, dear, not just before we eat,' said Mother.

'How about leaning against the cliff?' suggested Margo.

'That's a brain-wave,' said Mother. 'Over there, in that sort of little sheltered nook.'

As she started across the shingle towards it, a fairly large chunk of the cliff came away and fell to the beach with a crash, to be followed by a hissing waterfall of sand.

'Thank you,' said Larry. 'If you sit there, you sit alone. I have no desire to be buried alive.'

'Look, there's a big, black rock in the middle of the beach,' said Leslie, 'perfect for leaning against.'

He hurried ahead and reached the rock. He threw down the things he was carrying, draped the rock with the rug, padded it with cushions, and had a suitable seat for Mother to sink on to when she had staggered across the shingle to his side. Larry sat down beside her, and the rest of us spread more rugs and sat down, unpacking the vast array of food.

'There's a very curious smell around here,' Larry complained, his mouth full of curry-puff.

'It's the seaweed,' explained Leslie. 'It always pongs a bit.'

'It's supposed to be very healthy for you,' said Margo. 'Anywhere that smells of seaweed is supposed to be good for the lungs.'

'I wouldn't have thought that this smell was good for the lungs,' complained Mother. 'It's a bit . . . well, it's a bit . . . strong.'

'It comes in waves,' said Larry. 'I suppose the wind is carrying it.'

'Oh, yes, I can smell it,' said Margo, closing her eyes and inhaling deeply. 'You can almost *feel* it doing your lungs good.'

'Well, it's not doing *my* lungs any good,' exclaimed Larry.

'The wind will probably change in a minute and blow it the other way,' put in Leslie cheerfully, cutting himself a large piece of game pie.

'I do hope so. It's a bit over-powering,' said Mother.

We ate for some time in silence, and then Larry sniffed.

'It seems to be getting stronger,' he observed.

'No, it's just the way the wind blows it,' answered Leslie.

Larry got to his feet and peered about.

'I don't see any seaweed,' he said, 'except right over there at the water's edge.'

He came over to where we were sitting and sniffed again.

'Well, no wonder *you're* not complaining,' he commented bitterly, 'there's hardly any smell over here. It seems to be concentrated where Mother and I are sitting.'

He went back to where Mother was sipping her wine and enjoying a Cornish pasty, and prowled around. Suddenly he let out such a cry of anguish and rage that everybody jumped, and Mother dropped her glass of wine into her lap.

'Great God Almighty, look!' roared Larry. 'Just look where that bloody fool Leslie's put us! No wonder we're being stunk out; we'll probably die of typhoid!'

'Larry, dear, I do wish you wouldn't shout like that,' complained Mother, mopping up the wine in her lap with her handkerchief. 'It's quite possible to say things in a calm way.'

'No, it isn't!' said Larry, violently. 'No one can keep calm in the face of this . . . this olfactory outrage!'

'What outrage, dear?' asked Mother.

'Do you know what you're leaning against?' he asked. 'Do you know what that back-rest is, that was chosen for you by your son?'

'What?' replied Mother, glancing nervously over her shoulder. 'It's a rock, dear.'

'It's not a rock,' said Larry, with dangerous calm, 'nor is it a pile of sand, a boulder, or a fossilized dinosaur's pelvis. It is nothing remotely geological. Do you know what you and I have been leaning against the last half hour?'

'What, dear?' asked Mother, now considerably alarmed.

'A horse,' replied Larry. 'The mortal remains of a ruddy great horse.'

'Rubbish!' said Leslie, incredulously. 'It's a rock.'

'Do rocks have teeth?' enquired Larry, sarcastically. 'Do they have eye sockets? Do they have the remains of ears and manes? I tell you – owing either to your malevolence or stupidity, your mother and I will probably be stricken with some fatal disease.'

Leslie got up and went to have a look, and I joined him. Sure enough, from one end of the rug protruded a head which undeniably had once belonged to a horse. All the fur had fallen off and the skin, through a motion in the sea water, had become dark brown and leathery. The fish and gulls had emptied the eye sockets, and the skin of the lips was drawn back in a snarl displaying the tombstone-like teeth, a discoloured yellow.

'How damned odd,' said Leslie. 'I could have sworn it was a rock.'

'It would save us all a considerable amount of trouble if you invested in some glasses,' remarked Larry with asperity.

'Well, how was I to know?' asked Leslie, belligerently. 'You don't expect a bloody, great, dead horse to be lying about on a beach, do you?'

'Fortunately, my knowledge of the habits of horses is limited,' answered Larry. 'For all I know, it may have suffered a heart attack while bathing. This in no way excuses your crass stupidity in turning its rotten corpse into a chaise-longue for me and Mother.'

'Bloody nonsense!' said Leslie. 'The thing looked like a rock. If it's a dead horse, it should look like one, not like a damn great rock. It's not my fault.'

'It not only looks like a dead horse, but it smells like one,' went on Larry. 'If your nasal membranes hadn't been, like your intellect, stunted from birth, you would have noticed the fact. The rich, ambrosial smell alone would have told you it was a horse.'

'Now, now, dears, don't quarrel over the horse,' pleaded Mother, who had retreated up-wind and was standing with a handkerchief over her nose.

'Look,' said Leslie angrily, 'I'll bloody well show you.'

He flung the cushions aside and whipped away the blanket to reveal the horse's blackened and semi-mummified body. Margo screamed. Of course, when you knew it was a horse, it was difficult to see it as anything else, but to do Leslie justice, with its legs half-buried in the shingle and only its blackened, leathery torso showing, it could be mistaken for a rock.

'There you are!' exclaimed Leslie triumphantly. 'It looks just like a rock.'

'It doesn't remotely resemble a rock,' said Larry coldly. 'It looks what it is – an extremely dead horse. If you mistook it for anything, one could only think it was one of the more senile members of the Jockey Club.'

'Are you going to spend all afternoon arguing over a dead horse?' asked Margo. 'Really! You men make me sick.'

'Yes, Larry, dear,' said Mother, 'let's move away from it and find another spot to finish lunch.'

'Let's send Leslie on ahead,' suggested Larry. 'Maybe this time he could rustle up a cow or a couple of sheep. Who knows what other odoriferous farmyard trophies await us? A drowned pig would be a tasty addition to our menu.'

'Larry, do stop it,' said Mother firmly. 'It's quite bad enough having that smell, without you talking like that.'

'It's not *my* fault,' answered Larry irritably, as we moved along the beach. 'It's Leslie's. He's the one who found that delicious, disintegrating Derby winner. He's the Burke and Hare of Lulworth Cove. Why don't you attack him?'

We moved further down the beach, and now, our appetites stimulated by the sea air, the lack of smell, and the quarrels that had grown out of the discovery of the dead horse, we attacked our victuals once again with relish. Presently, nicely sated with food, and having, perhaps, drunk a shade too much wine, we all fell asleep and slept long and soundly. It was owing to this that none of us noticed the change in the weather. I was the first to awaken. At first I thought we had slept so long that it was late evening, for the whole of the bay was dark and gloomy, but a glance at my watch showed that it was only five o'clock. A quick look upwards and I saw why it appeared to be later. When we had gone to sleep, the sky had been a pale but bright blue, and the sea was sparkling, but now the sky was almost slate-coloured and the sea had turned a dark indigo in sympathy with it, and moved sullenly under sudden gusts and eddies of wind. Looking in the direction which the clouds were coming, I could see the horizon was as black as pitch, with shreds of lightning running through it, and to my ears came the not-too-distant rumble of thunder. Hastily, I gave the alarm, and the family sat up, bleary-eyed and half asleep. It took them a moment or so to assimilate the meteorological *volte face* that had taken place.

'Oh, dear,' said Mother, 'and the Air Ministry roof did promise . . .'

'This is an *awful* country,' complained Larry. 'Only a full-blooded masochist would enjoy living here. Everything in the place is a mortification of the flesh, from the cooking to the licensing laws, from the women to the weather.'

'We'd better get back to the car quickly. It's going to teem down in a minute,' said Leslie.

Hastily, we bundled up our goods and chattels and boxes and bags, and made our way along the beach. Arguing about the dead horse had distracted us, and we had moved further round the bay than we had meant to. Now we had quite a long walk back to the car. Before we were half-way there, the rain started. A few fat drops hit us at intervals and then, as if the rain had been getting the range, the clouds above us seemed simply to open like a trap door and the rain fell in what can only be described as a solid blanket. Within seconds, we were all drenched to the skin. The rain was icy. With chattering teeth, we ran up the hill to the Rolls, where the next of our misfortunes became apparent. Jack, beguiled by the sunlight, had left the hood back so that the inside of the Rolls was awash.

'God damn it!' bellowed Larry, raising his voice above the roar of the rain, 'does nobody use any intelligence around here?'

'How was I supposed to know it was going to rain?' asked Jack, aggrievedly.

'Because it always bloody does in this sponge of an island,' answered Larry.

Leslie and Jack were trying to get the hood up, but it soon became apparent that for some reason it was refusing to function.

'It's no good,' panted Leslie at last, 'we can't shift it. We'll just have to sit in the car and drive like hell to the nearest shelter.'

'Splendid!' said Larry. 'I've always wanted to be driven in an open car through a monsoon.'

'Oh, stop moaning, for heaven's sake,' snapped Leslie. 'We're all going to get equally wet.'

We piled into the Rolls, and Jack started her up. At first, in order to try to get us to shelter as quickly as possible, he drove fast, but soon, the cries and roars from the back, made him slow down, for to travel at any speed turned the rain into a stinging whip across one's face. We had progressed perhaps half a mile, when a familiar shuddering sensation made it clear to us all that we had a puncture. Cursing, Jack eased the Rolls to a standstill, and he and Leslie changed the wheel, while the rest of us sat in sodden silence, and the rain beat down. Margo's hair, so carefully prepared for the occasion, now hung in rat's tails about her face. Mother looked as though she'd just finished swimming the Atlantic single-handed, while Larry was probably in the worst condition of all. He'd put the ear-flaps down on his deer-stalker, but a steady stream of water, like a miniature Niagara, flowed off the peak of his hat and into his lap. The thick tweed of his coat absorbed water with the eagerness and completeness of a Saharan sand-dune. The coat was heavy in itself, but now it had absorbed some ten gallons of rain water, it hung round Larry like a suit of damp armour.

'What *I* want to know, Mother, is what you've got against me?' he remarked, as Jack and Leslie got into the car and we started off again.

'Whatever do you mean, dear?' asked Mother. 'I've got nothing against you. Don't be silly.'

'I can't believe that this is all fortuitous,' said Larry. 'It seems too well planned, as if you had some deep, psychological urge to destroy me. Why didn't you simply put a pillow over my face when I was in my pram? Why wait until I'm in my prime?'

'You do talk nonsense, Larry,' said Mother. 'If a stranger heard you talking like that, he'd think you meant it.'

'I *do* mean it,' exclaimed Larry. 'Never mind; my publishers are going to love the publicity; "Famous Novelist killed by Mother. 'I did it because I thought he was suffering,' she said".'

'Oh, do be quiet, Larry!' said Mother. 'You make me cross when you talk like that.'

'Well, the picnic was your idea,' Larry pointed out.

'But the Air Ministry roof . . .' Mother began.

'Spare me,' pleaded Larry. 'If you mention the Air Ministry roof once again, I shall scream. One can only hope they have all been struck by lightning.'

We had now reached the top of the cliffs. It was almost as dark as twilight, and the driving curtains of rain were pushed and trembled by gusts of wind so that one could not see more than a short distance with any clarity. A flash of golden lightning, accompanied by an enormous clap of thunder right overhead, made both Mother and Margo squeak with apprehension.

It was at that moment that we got our second puncture.

'Well,' said Jack, philosophically, as he pulled the car into the side of the road. 'That's it.'

There was a short silence.

'What do you mean: "that's it"?' asked Larry. 'Why don't you change the wheel? It may have escaped your notice, but it's still raining in the back here.'

'Can't,' replied Jack, succinctly. 'We've only got one spare.'

'Only one spare?' cried Larry, incredulously. 'Dear God! What organization! What planning! Do you realize that if Stanley had carried on like this he'd still be looking for Livingstone?'

'Well, I can't help it,' said Jack. 'We've used up our spare. You don't expect to get two punctures – one on top of the other.'

'The art of life is to be prepared for the unexpected,' said Larry.

'Well this *is* unexpected,' replied Margo. 'If you're so clever, you deal with it.'

'I will,' said Larry, to our surprise. 'When surrounded by morons the only thing to do is to take charge.'

So saying, he climbed laboriously out of the car.

'Where are you going, dear?' asked Mother.

'Over there,' said Larry, pointing. 'There is a man in a field. Don't ask me what he is doing in the field in the pouring rain; he's probably the village idiot. But from him I might ascertain where the nearest cottage or hostelry is with a telephone, and we can walk there and phone for a breakdown van.'

'That *is* clever of you,' said Mother, admiringly.

'Not really,' replied Larry. 'It's just that when you are surrounded on all sides by stupidity, any logical decision seems like a stroke of genius.'

He marched off down the road, and I followed him, determined not to miss anything.

We reached the field, on the far side of which was the man,

pacing about among the rows of some newly-emerging crop, whistling cheerily to himself. His shoulders were protected from the rain by a sack, and another one was draped over his head. Now and then he'd pause, bend down, examine a plant carefully, and then pull it up. I began to wonder whether he was the village idiot. We made our way towards him, between the furrows. The dark earth was as sticky as molasses and long before we reached him, both Larry and I were carrying some five pounds of soil on each shoe.

'What with my coat weighing about eight-hundred pounds, and the mud on my shoes, I might well suffer a cardiac arrest,' panted Larry.

'Hello, there!' I called to the man as soon as we were within ear-shot. He straightened up and looked at us, mud-covered, dripping.

'Goo' arternoon,' he called.

'You'd think, with its meteorological history, that the English language could have thought up another greeting, wouldn't you?' said Larry. 'It's perfectly preposterous to say "good afternoon" on a day whose climatic conditions could make even Noah worry.'

As we reached the man, Larry became as charming as his ridiculous costume and dripping condition would allow.

'So sorry to worry you,' he said, 'but our car's broken down. I was wondering if you'd be kind enough to tell us where the nearest telephone is, so that we can telephone for a breakdown van to come?'

The man studied us carefully. He had tiny, twinkling blue eyes and a hawk-like nose set in a great slab of a face as russet as an autumn apple.

'Telephone?' he queried. 'There's no telephone 'ere-abouts. No call for 'un really, sur – no, not out 'ere.'

'Yes, I understand,' went on Larry patiently, 'but where's the nearest one?'

'Nearest one?' said the man. 'Nearest one . . . Now, let me

think . . . It's a good long time since I used the telephone, but it'll come to me presently . . . Now, Geoff Rogers, he's jist down the valley *this* way, but 'e 'asn't got one . . . nor hasn't Mrs Charlton, she's up *that* way . . . no, I think your best solution, sur, is to go to the cross roads and turn right. That'll bring you to "The Bull" – the pub, sur, they've got a telephone . . . Leastways, they 'ad one when I was there last spring.'

'I see,' said Larry. 'How do we get to the cross roads from here?'

'It's a tidy walk, sur,' said the man. 'A good three miles it be.'

'If you could just give us directions,' Larry suggested.

'It's a tidy walk – an' up 'ill most o' the way,' went on the man.

'Well,' answered Larry, 'that's not important. If you could just tell us which . . .'

'I could lend you Molly,' said the man. 'That 'ud be quicker.'

'I wouldn't dream of inconveniencing your wife . . .' Larry began, when the man interrupted with a bellow of laughter.

'My wife!' he crowed. 'My wife! Bless your soul, sur, but that's a laugh, and no mistake. Molly ain't my *wife*, bless you, sur. She's my 'orse.'

'Oh,' said Larry. 'Well, it's very kind of you but I haven't ridden for years, and we've already had one unfortunate experience with a horse today.'

'No, no. You couldn't ride 'er,' said the man. ''Ur pulls a trap.'

'Oh, I see,' said Larry. 'But, then, how do we get her back to you?'

'Oh, don' you worry about that, sur. You jist 'itch up ur reins nice and snug to the trap and she'll come back to me. Oh, aye, she always comes back to where I'm at. She's as good as a wife, sur, and that's no disrespect to my ol' woman. If I goes to the pub of a Saturday, an' 'as one too many, they puts me in the trap, sur, and Molly takes me 'ome without a word of a lie, sur.'

'A sagacious animal,' observed Larry. 'Will your trap carry six people?'

'Yes, sur, if you takes it slow, like – and a couple of you walks up the steep bits.'

So we went round behind the hedge, where we found Molly, covered in sacks, chewing thoughtfully at her nosebag. She was as sturdy as an Exmoor pony but twice as big; the trap was a nice one; there was plenty of room. The man unhitched Molly and handed the reins to Larry, who passed them hurriedly to me.

'You're supposed to be the zoologist of the family. You drive,' he instructed.

The man gave us directions which, like all directions in the country, were full of confusing details like 'pass the blasted fir tree on your left' and 'go straight past the sheep dip or round it if you prefer'. We made him repeat them twice to get them right, and then, thanking him profusely, climbed into the trap. Molly, who must have been chilly standing in the hedge, responded eagerly to my chirrups of encouragement, and we set off towards the road at a spanking trot. Our appearance was greeted with hilarity and disbelief by the family.

'What are you going to do with that? Give us a tow?' enquired Leslie.

'No,' said Larry austerely, 'this vehicle is to take us to shelter and to a telephone. If we tie some picnic knives to the wheels, Margo can pretend she's Boadicea, and with a bit of luck we can run down a villager and cut off his legs.'

After a certain amount of argument, we persuaded everyone to vacate the sodden Rolls for the equally sodden but more mobile trap. The rain had eased off now to a fine mizzle which, if anything, made you damper than a hard downpour. Molly, her ears back to hear my encouraging comments on her prowess, pulled with a will and we progressed at a rapid walk down the lanes. After some twenty minutes, we were in totally unfamiliar and uninhabited country.

'I do hope you know where we are going, dear,' said Mother, anxiously.

'Of course I do,' answered Larry, impatiently. 'The man's instructions are burnt on my brain in letters of fire. Here, Gerry, turn right there, at that oak tree, and then second left.'

We progressed some distance in silence, and then we reached a cross roads without benefit of a signpost. Before Larry could give instructions, Molly, of her own volition, had turned to the left.

'There you are,' said Larry in triumph, 'the horse agrees with me. Even the dumb beasts of the field recognize a born leader. Anyway, her owner probably frequents this pub, so she knows the way.'

We plunged into a piece of damp and dripping woodland, where the wood pigeons clapped their wings at us and magpies clucked suspiciously. The road wound to and fro through the rain-soaked trees.

'Very soon now we'll reach this wonderful old country pub,' said Larry, waxing poetical. 'There'll be a huge, wood fire to warm our outsides, and a huge hot whisky and lemon to warm our insides. The landlord, a humble peasant, will leap to do our bidding, and while we are roasting by the fire . . .'

Here, we rounded a corner and Larry's voice died away. Fifty yards ahead of us, squatting in the mud, was the Rolls.

Molly may have had her failings, but she knew her way back to her master.

THE MAIDEN VOYAGE

However glib you are with words, your brain is inclined to falter if you try to describe the Piazza San Marco in Venice under a full daffodil-yellow summer moon. The buildings look as though they have been made out of crumbling over-sweet nougat in the most beautiful shades of browns and reds and subtle autumn pinks. You can sit and watch, fascinated, for the tiny tellers, Moorish figures, that come out and strike the big bell on St Mark's cathedral at every quarter, so that it echoes and vibrates around the huge square.

On this particular evening, it was as ravishing as only Venice could be, spoiled only by the conglomeration of my belligerent family, clustered around two tables which were bestrewn with drinks and tiny plates of appetisers. Unfortunately, it had been my mother's idea and, as had happened throughout her life, what she had produced as a treat had already, even at this early stage, started turning into a fiasco that was edging her slowly but relentlessly towards that pillory that all families keep for their parents.

'I wouldn't mind if you had had the decency to *tell* me in advance. I could, at least, have risked death travelling by air,' said my elder brother, Larry, looking despondently at one of the many glasses that an irritatingly happy waiter had put in front of him. 'But what in heaven's name possessed you to go and book us all on a *Greek* ship for three days? I mean, it's as stupid as deliberately booking on the *Titanic*.'

'I thought it would be more cheerful, and the Greeks are such good sailors,' replied my mother, defensively. 'Anyway, it's her maiden voyage.'

'You always cry wolf before you're hurt,' put in Margo. 'I think it was a brilliant idea of Mother's.'

'I must say, I agree with Larry,' said Leslie, with the obvious reluctance that we all shared in agreeing with our elder brother. 'We all know what Greek ships are like.'

'Not *all* of them, dear,' said Mother. '*Some* of them must be all right.'

'Well, there's damn all we can do about it now,' concluded Larry gloomily. 'You've committed us to sail on this bloody craft, which I have no doubt would have been rejected by the Ancient Mariner in his cups.'

'Nonsense, Larry,' said Mother. 'You always exaggerate. The man at Cook's spoke very highly of it.'

'He said the bar was full of life,' cried Margo triumphantly.

'God almighty,' exclaimed Leslie.

'And to dampen our pagan spirits,' agreed Larry, 'the most revolting selection of Greek wines, which all taste as though they have been forced from the reluctant jugular vein of some hermaphrodite camel.'

'Larry, don't be so disgusting,' said Margo.

'Look,' protested Larry vehemently, 'I have been dragged away from France on this ill-fated attempt to revisit the scenes of our youth, much against my better judgement. Already I am beginning to regret it, and we've only just got as far as Venice, for God's sake. Already I'm curdling what remains of my liver with Lacrima Christi instead of good, honest Beaujolais. Already my senses have been assaulted in every restaurant by great mounds of spaghetti, like some sort of awful breeding ground for tapeworms, instead of Charolais steaks.'

'Larry, I do wish you wouldn't talk like that,' said my

mother. 'There's no need for vulgarity.'

In spite of the three bands, all playing different tunes at different corners of the great square, the vocalization of the Italians and tourists, and the sleepy crooning of the somnambulistic pigeons, it seemed that half of Venice was listening, entranced, to our private family row.

'It will be perfectly all right when we are on board,' said Margo. 'After all, we *will* be among the Greeks.'

'I think that's what Larry's worried about,' commented Leslie gloomily.

'Well,' said Mother, trying to introduce an air of false confidence into the proceedings, 'we should be going. Taking one of those vaporiser things down to the docks.'

We paid our bill, straggled down to the Canal and climbed on board one of the motor launches which my mother, with her masterly command of Italian, insisted on calling a vaporiser. The Italians, being less knowledgeable, called them vaporettos. Venice was a splendid sight as we chugged our way down the Canal, past the great houses, past the rippling reflections of the lights in the water. Even Larry had to admit that it was a slight improvement on the Blackpool illuminations. We were landed eventually at the docks which, like docks everywhere in the world, looked as though they had been designed (in an off moment) by Dante while planning his Inferno. We huddled in puddles of phosphorescent light that made us all look like something out of an early Hollywood horror film and completely destroyed the moonlight, which was by now silver as a spider's web. Our gloom was not even lightened by the sight of Mother's diminutive figure attempting to convince three rapacious Venetian porters that we did not need any help with our motley assortment of luggage. It was an argument conducted in basic English.

'We English. We no speak Italian,' she cried in tones of despair, adding a strange flood of words which consisted of Hindustani, Greek, French and German, none of which bore any relation to each other. This was my mother's way of communication with any foreigner, be they Aborigine or Eskimo, but it failed to do more than momentarily lighten our gloom.

We stood and contemplated those bits of the Canal which led out into our section of the dock. Suddenly there slid into view a ship which, even by the most land-lubberish standards, could never have been mistaken for seaworthy. At some time in her career, she had been used as a species of reasonably-sized inshore steamer but even in those days, when she had been virginal and freshly painted, she could not have been beautiful. Now, sadly lacking in any of the trappings that, in that ghastly phosphorescent light, might have made her turn into a proud ship, there was nothing. Fresh paint had not come her way for a number of years and there were large patches of rust, like unpleasant sores and scabs, all along her sides. Like a woman on excessively high-heeled shoes who had had the misfortune to lose one of the heels, she had a heavy list to starboard. Her totally unkempt air was bad enough, but the final indignity was exposed as she turned to come alongside the docks. It was an enormous tattered hole in her bows that would have admitted a pair of Rolls-Royces side by side. This terrible defloration was made worse by the fact that no first-aid of any description, even of the most primitive kind, had been attempted. The plates on her hull curved inwards where they had been crushed, like a gigantic chrysanthemum. Struck dumb, we watched her come alongside; there, above the huge hole in her bows, was her name: the *Poseidon*.

'Dear God!' breathed Larry.

'She's appalling,' said Leslie, the more nautical member of our family. 'Look at that list.'

'But it's *our* boat,' squeaked Margo. 'Mother, it's our boat!'

'Nonsense, dear, it can't be,' said my mother, readjusting her spectacles and peering hopefully up at the boat as it loomed above us.

'Three days on this,' said Larry. 'It will be *worse* than the

Ancient Mariner's experience, mark my words.'

'I do hope they are going to do something about that hole,' said Mother worriedly, 'before we put out to sea.'

'What do you expect them to do? Stuff a blanket into it?' asked Larry.

'But surely the Captain's *noticed* it,' said Mother bewildered.

'I shouldn't think that even a Greek captain could have been oblivious of the fact that they have, quite recently, given something a fairly sharp tap,' said Larry.

'The waves will get in,' moaned Margo. 'I don't want waves in my cabin. My dresses will all be ruined.'

'I should think all the cabins are under water by now,' observed Leslie.

'Our snorkels and flippers will come in handy,' said Larry. '*What* a novelty to have to swim down to dinner. *How* I shall enjoy it all.'

'Well, as soon as we get on board you must go up and have a word with the Captain,' decided Mother. 'It's just possible that he wasn't on board when it happened, and no one's told him.'

'Really, Mother, you do annoy me,' said Larry irritably. 'What do you expect me to say to the man? "Pardon me, Kyrie Capitano, sir, but did you know you've got death-watch beetle in your bows?" '

'Larry, you always complicate things,' complained Mother. 'You know I can't speak Greek or I'd do it.'

'Tell him I don't want waves in my cabin,' insisted Margo.

'As we are due to leave tonight, they couldn't possibly mend it anyway,' observed Leslie.

'Exactly,' said Larry. 'But Mother seems to think that I am some sort of reincarnation of Noah.'

'Well, I shall have something to say about it when I get on board,' said Mother belligerently, as we made our way up the gangway.

At the head of the gangway, we were met by a romantic-looking Greek steward (with eyes as soft and melting as black pansies) wearing a crumpled and off-grey white suit, with most of the buttons missing. From his tarnished epaulettes, he appeared to be the Purser, and his smiling demand for passports and tickets was so redolent of garlic that Mother reeled back against the rails, her query about the ship's bows stifled.

'Do you speak English?' asked Margo, gamely rallying her olfactory nerves more rapidly than Mother.

'Small,' he replied, bowing.

'Well, I don't want waves in my cabin,' said Margo firmly. 'It will ruin my clothes.'

'Everything you want we give,' he answered. 'If you want wife, I give you *my* wife. She . . .'

'No, no,' exclaimed Margo, 'the *waves*. You know . . . water.'

'Every cabeen has having hot and cold running showers,' he said with dignity. 'Also there is bath or nightcloob having dancing and wine and water.'

'I do wish you'd stop laughing and help us, Larry,' said Mother, covering her nose with her handkerchief to repel the odour of garlic, which was so strong that one got the impression it was like a shimmering cloud round the Purser's head.

Larry pulled himself together and in fluent Greek (which delighted the Purser) elicited, in rapid succession, the information that the ship was not sinking, that there were no waves in the cabins, and that the Captain knew all about the accident as he had been responsible for it. Wisely, Larry did not pass on this piece of information to Mother. While Mother and Margo were taken in a friendly and aromatic manner down to the cabins by the Purser, the rest of us then followed his instructions as to how to get to the bar.

This, when we located it, made us all speechless. It looked like the mahogany-lined lounge of one of the drearier London clubs. Great chocolate-coloured leather chairs and couches cluttered the place, interspersed with formidable fumed-oak tables. Dotted about were huge Benares brass bowls in which sprouted tattered, dusty palm trees. There was, in the midst of this funereal splendour, a minute parquet floor for dancing, flanked on one side by the small bar containing a virulent assortment of drinks, and on the other by a small raised dais, surrounded by a veritable forest of potted palms. In the midst of this, enshrined like flies in amber, were three lugubrious musicians in frock coats, celluloid dickies, and cummerbunds that would have seemed dated in about 1890. One played on an ancient upright piano and tuba, one played a violin with much professional posturing, and the third doubled up on the drums and trombone. As we entered, this incredible trio was playing 'The Roses of Picardy' to an entirely empty room.

'I can't bear it,' said Larry. 'This is not a ship, it's a sort of floating Cadena Café from Bournemouth. It'll drive us all mad.'

At Larry's words, the band stopped playing and the leader's face lit up in a gold-toothed smile of welcome. He gestured at his two colleagues with his bow and they also bowed and smiled. We three could do no less, and so we swept them a courtly bow before proceeding to the bar. The band launched itself with ever greater frenzy into 'The Roses of Picardy' now that it had an audience.

'Please give me,' Larry asked the barman, a small wizened man in a dirty apron, 'in one of the largest glasses you possess, an ouzo that will, I hope, paralyse me.'

The barman's walnut face lit up at the sound of a foreigner who could not only speak Greek but was rich enough to drink so large an ouzo.

'*Amessos*, kyrie,' he said. 'Will you have it with water or ice?'

'One lump of ice,' Larry stipulated. 'Just enough to blanch its cheeks.'

'I'm sorry, kyrie, we have no ice,' said the barman, apologetically.

Larry sighed a deep and long-suffering sigh.

'It is only in Greece,' he said to us in English, 'that one has this sort of conversation. It gives one the feeling that one is in such close touch with Lewis Carroll that the barman might be the Cheshire cat in disguise.'

'Water, kyrie?' asked the barman, sensing from Larry's tone that he was not receiving approbation but rather censure.

'Water,' said Larry, in Greek, 'a tiny amount.'

The barman went to the massive bottle of ouzo, as clear as gin, poured out a desperate measure, and then went to the little sink and squirted water in from the tap. Instantly, the ouzo turned the colour of watered milk and we could smell the aniseed from where we were standing.

'God, that's a strong one,' said Leslie. 'Let's have the same.'

I agreed. The glasses were set before us. We raised them in toast:

'Well, here's to the *Marie Celeste* and all the fools who sail in her,' said Larry, and took a great mouthful of ouzo. The next minute he spat it out in a flurry that would have done credit to a dying whale, and reeled back against the bar, clasping his throat, his eyes watering.

'Ahhh!' he roared. 'The bloody fool's put bloody *hot water* in it!'

Nurtured as we had been among the Greeks, we were inured to the strange behaviour they indulged in, but for a Greek to put boiling water in his national drink, was, we felt, carrying eccentricity too far.

'Why did you put hot water in the ouzo?' asked Leslie belligerently.

'Because we have no cold,' said the barman, surprised that Leslie should not have worked out this simple problem in logic for himself. 'That is why we have no ice. This is the maiden voyage, kyrie, and that is why we have nothing but hot water in the bar.'

'I don't believe it,' said Larry brokenly. 'I just don't believe it. A maiden voyage and the ship's got a bloody great hole in her bows, a Palm Court Orchestra of septuagenarians, and nothing but hot water in the bar.'

At that moment Mother appeared, looking distinctly flustered.

'Larry, I want to speak to you,' she panted.

Larry looked at her. 'What have you found? An iceberg in the bunk?' he asked.

'Well, there's a cockroach in the cabin. Margo threw a bottle of Eau de Cologne at it, and it broke, and now the whole place smells like a hairdresser's. I don't think it killed the cockroach either,' said Mother.

'Well,' rejoined Larry. 'I'm delighted you have been having fun. Have a red-hot ouzo to round off the start of this riotous voyage.'

'No, I didn't come here to drink.'

'You surely didn't come to tell me about an Eau de Cologne-drenched cockroach?' asked Larry in surprise. 'Your conversation is getting worse than the Greeks for eccentricity.'

'No, it's Margo,' Mother hissed. 'She went to the you-know-where and she's got the slot jammed.'

'The "you-know-where"? Where's that?'

'The lavatory, of course. You know perfectly well what I mean.'

'I don't know what you expect me to do,' said Larry. 'I'm not a plumber.'

'Can't she climb out?' enquired Leslie.

'No,' said Mother. 'She's tried, but the hole at the top is much too small, and so is the hole at the bottom.'

'But at least there are holes,' Larry pointed out. 'You need air in a Greek lavatory in my experience and we can feed her through them during the voyage.'

'Don't be so stupid, Larry,' said Mother. 'You've got to do something.'

'Try putting another coin in the slot thing,' suggested Leslie. 'That sometimes does it.'

'I did,' said Mother. 'I put a lira in but it still wouldn't work.'

'That's because it's a Greek lavatory and will only accept drachmas,' Larry pointed out. 'Why didn't you try a pound note? The rate of exchange is in its favour.'

'Well, I want you to get a stewardess to help her out,' said Mother. 'She's been in there ages. She can't stay all night. Supposing she banged her elbow and fainted? You know she's always doing that.' Mother tended to look on the black side of things.

'In my experience of Greek lavatories,' said Larry judiciously, 'you generally faint immediately upon entering without the need to bang your elbow.'

'Well, for heaven's sake *do* something!' cried Mother. 'Don't just stand there drinking.'

Led by her, we eventually found the lavatory in question. Leslie, striding in masterfully, rattled the door.

'Me stuck. Me English,' shouted Margo from behind the door. 'You find stewardess.'

'I know that, you fool. It's me, Leslie,' he growled.

'Go out at once. It's a ladies' lavatory,' said Margo.

'Do you want to get out or not? If you do, shut up!' retorted Leslie belligerently.

He fiddled ineffectually with the door, swearing under his breath.

'I do wish you wouldn't use bad language, dear,' protested Mother. 'Remember, you *are* in the ladies'.'

'There should be a little knob thing on the inside which you pull,' said Leslie. 'A sort of bolt thing.'

'I've pulled everything,' rejoined Margo indignantly. 'What do you think I've been doing in here for the last hour?'

'Well, pull it again,' suggested Leslie, 'while I push.'

'All right, I'm pulling,' said Margo.

Leslie humped his powerful shoulders and threw himself at the door.

'It's like a Pearl White serial,' said Larry, sipping the ouzo that he had thoughtfully brought with him and which had by now cooled down. 'If you're not careful we'll have another hole in the hull.'

'It's no good,' said Leslie panting. 'It's too tough. We'll have to get a steward or something.'

He went off in search of someone with mechanical knowledge.

'I do wish you'd hurry,' said Margo, plaintively. 'It's terribly oppressive in here.'

'Don't faint,' cried Mother in alarm. 'Try to regulate your breathing.'

'And don't bang your elbows,' Larry added.

'Oh, Larry, you do make me cross,' said Mother. 'Why can't you be sensible?'

'Well, shall I go and get her a hot ouzo? We can slide it in under the door,' he suggested helpfully.

He was saved from Mother's ire by the arrival of Leslie, bringing in tow a small and irritated puppet-like man with a lugubrious face.

'Always the ladies is doing this,' he said to Mother, shrugging expressive shoulders. 'Always they are getting catched. I show you. It is easy. Why woman not learn?'

He went to the door, fiddled with it for a moment, and it flew open.

'Thank God,' said Mother, as Margo appeared in the doorway. But before she could emerge into the bosom of her family, the little man held up a peremptory hand.

'Back!' he commanded, masterfully. 'I teaches you.'

Before we could do anything intelligent, he had pushed Margo back into the lavatory and slammed the door shut.

'What's he doing?' squeaked Mother in alarm. 'What's he doing, that little man? Larry, do something.'

'It's all right, Mother,' shouted Margo, 'he's showing me how to do it.'

46

'How to do what?' asked Mother, alarmed.

There was a long and ominous silence, eventually broken by a flood of Greek oaths.

'Margo, you come out of there at once,' ordered Mother, considerably alarmed.

'I can't,' wailed Margo. 'He's locked us both in.'

'Disgusting man,' cried Mother, taking command. 'Hit him dear, hit him. Larry, you go for the Captain.'

'I mean, he can't open the door either,' said Margo.

'Please to find Purser,' wailed the little man. 'Please finding Purser for opening door.'

'Well, where do we find him?' asked Leslie.

'It's too ridiculous,' said Mother. 'Are you all right? Stand well away from him, dear.'

'You find Purser in Purser's office, first deck,' yelled the imprisoned man.

The ensuing scene, to anyone who does not know the Greek temperament and their strange ability to change a perfectly normal situation into something so complicated that it leaves the Anglo Saxon mind unhinged, may find what followed incredible. We, knowing the Greeks, did also. Leslie returned with the Purser, who not only added to the redolence of the Ladies' with his garlic, but in quick succession complimented Larry on drinking ouzo and Leslie on his Greek accent, soothed Mother with a large carnation plucked from behind his ear, and then turned such a blast of invective on the poor little man locked up with my sister that one expected the solid steel door to melt. He rushed at it and pounded with his fists and kicked it several times. Then he turned to Mother and bowed.

'Madam,' he said, smiling, 'no alarm. Your daughter is safe with a virgin.'

This remark confused Mother completely. She turned to me for explanation, as Larry, knowing this sort of fracas of old, had repaired to the bar to get drinks. I said I thought he meant she would be as safe *as* a virgin.

47

'He can't mean *that*,' she said suspiciously. 'She's got two children.'

I began to lose my bearings slightly as one always seemed to do when confused by the Greeks. I had just taken an unwisely deep breath to embark on an elaboration for my Mother, when I was mercifully stopped by the arrival of three fellow passengers, all large, big-bosomed, thick-legged peasant ladies, with heavy moustaches and black bombazine dresses three times too small, smelling of garlic, some sickly scent, and perspiration in equal quantities. They elbowed their way between Mother and myself and entered the lavatory. Seeing the Purser still dancing with rage and pounding on the door, they paused like massive war-horses that have scented battle.

Any other nationality would have complained about the Purser's presence in this shrine to womanhood, let alone mine as a foreigner's, but this is where the Greeks so delightfully differ from other races. They knew it was a SITUATION with capital letters, and this above all is what Greeks love. The presence of three men (if you include the invisible one closeted with Margo) in their lavatory was as nothing compared to the SITUATION.

Their eyes glittered, their moustaches wiffled and, a solid wall of eager flesh, they enveloped the Purser and demanded to know what was afoot. As usual in a SITUATION, everyone spoke at once. The temperature in the Ladies' went up to something like seventy degrees and the volume of sound made one's head spin, like playing the noisier bits of the Ride of the Valkyries in an iron barrel.

Having grasped the elements of the SITUATION from the harassed Purser, the three powerful ladies, each built on the lines of a professional wrestler, swept him out of the way with scarlet-tipped spade-shaped hands and proceeded to lift up their skirts. With deafening cries of 'Oopah, oopah' they charged the lavatory door. Their combined weights must have amounted to some sixty stone of flesh and bone, but the door was stalwart and the three ladies fell in a tangle of limbs on the floor. They got to their feet with some difficulty and then argued among themselves as to the best way to break down a lavatory door.

One of them, the least heavy of the three, demonstrated her idea – an ideal method – against one of the other lavatory doors. This, unfortunately, was not on the latch and so she crashed through at surprising speed and received a nasty contusion upon her thigh by crashing full tilt into the lavatory pan. Although it had not proved her point, she was very good-natured about it, especially as at that moment Larry arrived accompanied by the barman carrying a tray of drinks.

For a time we all sipped ouzo companionably, toasted each other, and asked if we were all married and how many children we had. Fresh interest in the SITUATION was aroused by the arrival of Leslie with what appeared to be the ship's carpenter for whom he had gone in search. Everyone now forgot their drinks and expounded their theories to the carpenter, all of which he disagreed with, with the air of one who knows. He then, like a magician, rolled up his sleeves and approached the door. Silence fell. He produced a minute screwdriver from his pocket and inserted it into a minute hole. There was a click and a gasp of admiration, and the door flew open. He stood back and spread his hands like a conjuror.

The first little man and Margo emerged like survivors from the Black Hole of Calcutta. The poor little man was seized by the Purser and pounded and pummelled and shaken, while being roundly abused. The carpenter, at this stage, took over. After all, he had opened the door. We listened to him with respect as he expounded the cunning mechanism of locks in general and this one in particular. He drained an ouzo and waxed poetic on locks, which were his hobby it appeared. With his little screwdriver or a hairpin or a bent nail or, indeed, a piece of plastic, he could open any lock. He took the first little man and the Purser by the wrist and led them into the lavatory like lambs to the slaughter. Before we could stop them, he had slammed the door shut. My family and the three fat ladies waited with bated breath. There were strange scrapings and clickings, then a long pause. This was followed by a torrent of vituperation from the Purser and the Steward, mixed with confused excuses and explanations from the lock expert. As we furtively crept away, the three ladies were preparing to charge the door again.

So ended scene one of the maiden voyage.

I draw a veil over the increasing irritability of my family that evening because, for some strange Greek reason of protocol, dinner could not be served until the Purser had been released. This took a considerable time since the constant assaults to which the door had been subjected had irretrievably damaged the lock and they had to wait until the Bosun could be retrieved, from some carousal ashore, to saw through the hinges. We eventually gave up waiting, went ashore, had a quick snack, and then retired to our respective cabins in a morbid state of mind.

The following morning, we went down to the dining-room and tried to partake of breakfast. The years had mercifully obliterated our memories of the average Greek's approach to cuisine. There are, of course, places in Greece where one can eat well, but they have to be searched for and are as rare as unicorns. Greece provides most of the ingredients for good cooking but the inhabitants are generally so busy arguing that they have no time left to pursue the effete paths of *haute cuisine*.

The four young waiters in the dining saloon were no exception and kept up an incessant and noisy warfare with each other like a troupe of angry magpies disputing a titbit. The decor, if that is not too strong a word, followed that of the bar, which we had now discovered was called the Night-Cloob. Fumed oak pervaded all. The brasswork had not been polished with more than a superficial interest in its brightness and the

50

tables were covered with off-white table-cloths covered with the ghosts of stains that some remote laundry in Piraeus had not quite succeeded in exorcising. Mother surreptitiously but determinedly polished all her cutlery on her handkerchief and exhorted us to do the same. The waiters, since we were the only people there for breakfast, saw no reason to disturb their bickering until Larry, tried beyond endurance, bellowed, '*Se parakalo!*' in such vibrant tones that Mother dropped three pieces of Margo's cutlery on the floor. The waiters ceased their cacophony immediately and surrounded our table with the most healthy obsequiousness. Mother, to her delight, found that one of the waiters, an ingratiating young man, had spent some time in Australia and had a rudimentary knowledge of English.

'Now,' she said, beaming at her protégé, 'what I would like is a nice, large pot of hot tea. Make sure the pot is warmed and the water is boiling, and none of those tea-bag things that make one shudder when one refills the pot.'

'I'm always reminded of the Bramaputra after an epidemic,' said Larry.

'Larry, dear, please, not at breakfast,' remonstrated Mother, and continued to the waiter, 'and then I shall have some grilled tomatoes on toast.'

We sat back expectantly. After years of experience, Mother had never given up a pathetic hope that she would one day find a Greek who would understand her requirements. As was to be expected, the waiter had let Mother's instructions regarding the tea pass unnoticed. Tea grew in tea-bags, and any attempt to tamper with nature would, he felt, involve dire consequences for all concerned. However, Mother had now introduced into his life a complication, a species of food unknown to him.

'Gill-ed tomatoes?' he queried uncomfortably. 'What is?'

'Gilled tomatoes,' echoed Mother, 'I mean grilled tomatoes. You know, tomatoes grilled on toast.'

The waiter clung to the one sane thing in the world, toast.

'Madam want toast,' he said firmly, trying to keep Mother on the right track, 'tea and toast.'

'*And* tomatoes,' said Mother, enunciating clearly, 'grilled tomatoes.'

A faint bead of perspiration made itself apparent upon the waiter's brow.

'What is "gill-ed tomatoes", Madam?' he asked, thus bringing the thing full circle.

We had all relaxed around the table having ordered our breakfast, *sotto voce*, and now we watched Mother launch herself into battle.

'Well,' she explained. 'You know, um, tomatoes . . . those, those red things, like apples. No, no, I mean plums.'

'Madam want plums?' asked the boy, puzzled.

'No, no, *tomatoes*,' said Mother. 'Surely you know tomatoes?'

The gloom on the young Greek's face lightened. She wanted tomatoes.

'Yes, Madam,' he answered, smiling.

'There,' said Mother, triumphantly, 'well then, tomatoes grilled on toast.'

'Yes, Madam,' he said dutifully, and went away into the corner and communed with the Purser.

Greek gesticulations are remarkable for their force and expressiveness. Behind Mother's back we watched the shadow-play between the waiter and the Purser. The Purser obviously told him in no uncertain manner that if he didn't know what grilled tomatoes were he must go and ask. Disconsolately, the waiter approached to encounter Mother once again.

'Madam,' he said mournfully, 'how you make gill-ed?'

Mother, until then, had been under the impression that she had made a major breakthrough in the barriers that the Greeks kept putting up against her. She suddenly felt deflated.

'What is "gill-ed"?' she asked the waiter. 'I don't speak Greek.'

He looked flabbergasted. It had, after all, been Madam's idea in the first place. He felt that she was being unfair in now trying to lay the blame at his door. She had asked for 'gill-ed'; if she didn't know what 'gill-ed' was, who the hell did?

'Tomatoes Madam wants,' he said, starting all over again.

'On toast,' repeated Mother.

He wandered away moodily and had another altercation with the Purser, which ended in the Purser ordering him sternly to the kitchen.

'Really,' said Mother, 'one knows one's back in Greece because one can't get anything done properly.'

We waited for the next round. Basically, the rule in Greece is to expect everything to go wrong and to try to enjoy it whether it does or doesn't.

After a long interval, the waiter came back with the things we had ordered and plonked a pot of tea in front of Mother and a plate upon which there was a piece of bread and two raw tomatoes cut in half.

'But this is not what I ordered,' she complained. 'They're raw, and it's bread.'

'Tomatoes, Madam,' said the boy stubbornly. 'Madam say tomatoes.'

'But *grilled*,' protested Mother. 'You know, cooked.'

The boy just stared at her.

'Look,' said Mother, as one explaining to an idiot child, 'you make toast first, you understand? You make the toast.'

'Yes,' replied the boy dismally.

'All right, then,' said Mother. 'Then you put the tomatoes on the toast and you grill them. Understand?'

'Yes, Madam. You no want this?' he asked, gesturing at the plate of bread and tomatoes.

'No, not like that. Grilled,' said Mother.

The boy wandered off carrying the plate, and had another sharp altercation with the Purser, who was now harassed by the arrival of a lot of Greek passengers, including our fat ladies, all of whom were demanding attention.

We watched the waiter, fascinated, as he put the plate of tomatoes and bread on a table and then spread out a paper napkin with the air of a conjuror about to perform a very complicated trick. Our hypnotized gaze attracted the attention of Mother and Margo and they looked round in time to see the waiter place the bread and the tomatoes carefully in the middle of the napkin.

'What on earth is he doing?' asked Mother.

'Performing some ancient Greek rite,' explained Larry.

The waiter now folded up the napkin with the bread and tomatoes inside, and started across the saloon.

'He's not bringing them to me like that, is he?' asked Mother in amazement.

We watched entranced as he solemnly made his way across the saloon and laid his burden upon the big oil stove in the centre of it. Although it was spring, the weather was chilly, and so the stove had been lit and was, indeed, almost red hot and giving out a comforting heat. I think we all divined what he was going to do but could not quite conceive such an action being possible. Before our fascinated eyes he placed napkin, bread and tomatoes carefully on the glowing lid of the stove and then stepped back to watch. There was a moment's pause and the napkin burst into flames to be followed, almost immediately, by the bread. The waiter, alarmed that his novel form of cookery was not being effective, seized another napkin from a nearby table and tried to extinguish the blaze by throwing it over the top of the stove. The napkin, not unnaturally, caught fire too.

'I don't know what Greek delicacy that is,' said Larry, 'but it looks delicious, and cooked *almost* by the table, too.'

'The boy must be mad,' exclaimed Mother.

'I hope you're not going to eat them after all *that*,' said Margo. 'It doesn't look very hygienic.'

'It's the only really piquant way of doing tomatoes,' insisted Larry. 'And think what fun you'll have picking the bits of charred napkin out of your teeth afterwards.'

'Don't be so disgusting, Larry,' protested Mother. 'I'm certainly not eating that.'

Two other waiters had joined the first and all three were trying to beat out the flames with napkins. Bits of tomato and flaming toast flew in all directions, landing indiscriminately on tables and customers alike. One of our fat ladies of the night before was blotched with a succulent section of tomato, and an old gentleman ,who had just sat down, had his tie pinned to him with a piece of flaming toast like a red hot Indian arrow. The Purser, emerging from the kitchen, took in the situation at a glance. He seized a large jug of water and running forward, threw it over the stove. It certainly had the effect of extinguishing the flames, but all the closer tables were immediately enveloped in steam, and clouds spread over the dining saloon containing the blended scents of tomato, burnt bread and charred napkin.

'It smells just like minestrone,' said Larry. 'I do think after all the boy's efforts you ought to try just a little, Mother.'

'Don't be ridiculous, Larry,' cried Mother. 'They've all gone mad.'

'No,' said Leslie, 'they've all gone Greek.'

'The terms are synonymous,' observed Larry.

One waiter had now hit another for some inexplicable reason, the Purser was shaking the original waiter by his lapels and shouting in his face. The scene was further enlivened by vociferous cries of complaint and annoyance from the surrounding tables. The threatening gestures, the pushing, the rich invective, were fascinating to watch but, like all good things, they eventually ended with the Purser slapping the original waiter over the back of his head and the waiter ripping off his badge of office, his dingy white coat, and hurling it at the Purser, who threw it back at him and ordered him out of the saloon. He curtly told the other waiters to clean up the mess and made placating noises to all and sundry as he made his way over to our table. He stopped, drew himself up to his full height beside us, plucked a fresh carnation from his button-hole and put it in Mother's left hand, while seizing her right hand and kissing it gracefully.

'Madam,' he said, 'I am apologetic. We cannot give you grillid tomatoes. Anything else you want, we do, but grillid tomatoes, no.'

'Why not?' asked Larry, in a spirit of curiosity.

'Because the grill in the kitchen it is broken. You see,' he added by way of explanation, 'it is the maiden voyage.'

'It seems the most unmaidenly voyage to me,' commented Leslie.

'Tell me,' enquired Larry, 'why was the waiter trying to grill on that stove?'

'The boy very stupid,' said the Purser. 'We have only experienced personnel on this ship. He will be dismantled in Piraeus.'

'How do you dismantle a waiter?' asked Larry, fascinated.

'Larry, dear, the Purser is a very busy man, so don't let's keep him,' said Mother hastily. 'I'll just have a boiled egg.'

'Thank you,' replied the Purser with dignity and he bowed and disappeared into the kithcen.

'I would have settled for raw tomatoes if I'd been you,' said Larry. 'You saw what they did with the grilled tomatoes. I dread to think what they are going to do with the boiled eggs.'

'Nonsense, Larry,' answered Mother. 'There isn't anything they can do to spoil a boiled egg.'

She was wrong. When the eggs arrived (two of them, which were put before her ten minutes later), not only were they hard but they had been carefully deprived of their shells by loving but unwashed fingers.

'There!' exclaimed Larry. 'What a treat! Cooked to a turn and covered with fingerprints that Sherlock Holmes would have found irresistible.'

Mother had to conceal these strange avian relics in her bag and then throw them overboard after breakfast when she was

56

sure no one was looking, for, as she observed, we didn't want to hurt anyone's feelings.

'There's one thing to be said for it,' said Larry, watching Mother casting the eggs upon the waters. 'Three days on a diet of nothing but red-hot ouzo will render us slim as minnows and we'll all be as convivial as Bacchus by the time we land.'

But he was wrong too.

The evening meal was, by Greek standards, almost epicurean. There were three courses, the first of which was cold by intention, being an *hors d'oeuvre*, and the other two cold because they were served on cold plates accompanied by the usual altercation between the waiters. However, everything was edible and the only imbroglio was caused by Margo discovering a baby cuttlefish's eye in her *hors d'oeuvre*. We unwisely drank far too many bottles of Domestika and arose from the table unsteadily and benignly.

'You go night-cloob?' asked the Purser, as he bowed us out.

'Why not,' said Larry, struck by the idea. 'Let's go and have an orgy among the palms. Do you remember how to do the Lancers, Mother?'

'I'm not going to make an exhibition of myself,' replied Mother with dignity. 'But I will have a coffee and perhaps a small brandy.'

'To the evil depths of the palm enshrouded night-cloob, then,' said Larry, steering Mother rather unsteadily along the deck, 'where who knows what opium titillated oriental maidens await us. Did we bring a jewel for Margo's navel?'

As we had lingered over our meal, we found that the night club was in full swing. Our three fat ladies, and an assortment of other passengers, were, to the strains of a Viennese waltz, jostling for position on the minute square of parquet, like fish crowded in the tail end of a seine net. Although all the luxuriously uncomfortable chairs and sofas and tables appeared to be occupied, an eager steward materialized at our elbows and showed us to the most illuminated and conspicuous table and chairs in a place of honour. They were, we were told to our alarm and despondency, specially reserved for us by the Captain. We were just about to protest that we wanted a dim and obscure table when, unfortunately, the Captain himself appeared. He was one of those very dark, romantically melting Greeks, slightly on the fleshy side but giving the impression that this made him more nubile and attractive, in that curious way Levantines have.

'Madam,' he said, making it seem like a compliment, 'I am enchanted to have you and your most beautiful sister on board our ship on her maiden voyage.'

It was a remark that, had the Captain known it, was calculated to offend everyone. It made Mother think he was what she always used to call darkly 'one of those sort of men', while one could see that Margo, though fond of Mother, felt that there was some difference between her seventy-odd summers and Margo's well-preserved thirties. For a moment the Captain's fate hung in the balance; then Mother decided to forgive him as he was, after all, a foreigner, and Margo decided to forgive him because he was really rather handsome. Leslie judged him with suspicion, obviously feeling that the hole in the bows proved his nautical standards to be of a low order. Larry had reached that benign state of intoxication when everyone seemed tolerable. With the suavity of a professional head waiter, the Captain arranged us round the table, seating himself between Mother and Margo, and beamed at us, his gold fillings twinkling like fireflies in his dark face. He ordered a round of drinks and then, to Mother's horror, asked her for the first dance.

'Oh, no!' she said. 'I'm afraid my dancing days are quite over. I leave that sort of thing to my daughter.'

'But, Madam,' implored the Captain, 'you're my guest. You must dance.' So masterful was he that, to our astonishment, Mother – like a rabbit hypnotized by a stoat – rose and allowed him to escort her out on to the dance floor.

'But Mother hasn't danced since Dad died in nineteen-twenty-six,' gasped Margo.

'She's gone mad,' said Leslie gloomily. 'She'll have a heart attack and we'll have to bury her at sea.'

Being buried at sea had been her last choice anyway. Mother spent much of her time choosing places in which to be buried.

'She's more likely to be trampled to death, with those three enormous women about,' observed Larry. 'Fatal to attempt to get on to that floor. It's like entering an arena full of rogue elephants.'

Indeed, the floor was so packed that the couples were gyrating at an almost glacial slowness. The Captain, using Mother as a battering ram and aided by his broad shoulders, had managed to fight his way into the solid wall of flesh and he and Mother were now embedded in its depth. Mother, owing to her diminutive size, was impossible to see but we caught an occasional glimpse of the Captain's face and the twinkling of his teeth. Finally, the last liquid notes of 'Tales from the Vienna Woods' crashed out and the gasping, panting, sweating dancers left the floor. Mother, crumpled and purple in the face, was half carried back to our table by the beaming Captain. She sank into her chair, too breathless to speak, and fanned herself with her handkerchief.

'The waltz is a very good dance,' said the Captain, gulping his ouzo. 'And it is not only a good dance but it is good exercise also for all the muscles.'

He seemed oblivious to the fact that Mother, gasping, and with congested face, looked like someone who has just returned from a near fatal encounter with King Kong.

It was Margo's turn next but being younger and lighter on her feet and more agile than Mother, she survived rather better.

When she returned, Mother offered effusive thanks to the Captain for his hospitality but said she thought she ought to be getting to bed as she had had rather a busy day. She'd actually spent the day wrapped in blankets in a rickety deck chair complaining about the cold wind and the choppy sea. So she made a graceful retreat and was escorted to her cabin by Leslie. By the time he returned, Margo, using all her undoubted charms, had persuaded the Captain that, although Viennese waltzes were all right as a toning-up exercise, no Greek ship worthy of its name (and certainly not one on her maiden voyage) could ignore the cultural inheritance of Greece as embodied in her national dances. The Captain was much struck by both Margo and the scheme and, before we had orientated ourselves to the idea, had taken control of Greece's national heritage. He strode over to the septuagenarian band and demanded of them in loud tones what fine old cultural Greek tunes they knew. Tunes of the peasantry, of the people. Tunes that brought out both the wonders of Greece and the valour of her people, the poignancy of her history and the beauty of her architecture, the subtlety of her mythology, the sparkling brilliance that had led the world, tunes that would conjure up Plato, Socrates, the glory of Greeks past, present and future.

The violinist said they only knew one such tune and that was 'Never on Sunday'.

The Captain came as near to having an apoplectic fit as anyone I've ever seen. With veins throbbing in his temple he turned, threw out his arms, and addressed the assembled company. Had anyone, he asked, rhetorically, ever heard of a Greek band that did not know a Greek tune?

'Ummm,' said the crowd, as crowds do when presented with something they don't quite understand.

'Send for the Chief Officer!' roared the Captain. 'Where is Yanni Papadopoulos?'

So threatening did he look, standing in the middle of the dance floor with clenched fist and bared golden teeth, that the waiters went scurrying in search of the Chief Officer, who presently appeared, looking faintly alarmed, presumably fearing that another hole in the bows had appeared.

'Papadopoulos,' snarled the Captain, 'are not the songs of

Greece one of the best things about our cultural heritage?'

'Of course,' said Papadopoulos, relaxing slightly, since it did not seem from the conversation that his job was in jeopardy. It was obvious, he thought, that he was on safe ground. Even an unreasonable Captain could not blame him for the brilliance or otherwise of the musical heritage of Greece.

'Why you never tell me, then,' said the Captain, glowering fiendishly, 'that this band don't know any Greek tunes, eh?'

'They do,' said the Chief Officer.

'They don't,' said the Captain.

'But I've *heard* them,' protested the Chief Officer.

'Play what?' asked the Captain, ominously.

' "Never on Sunday",' said the Chief Officer triumphantly.

The word 'excreta' in Greek is a splendid one for spitting out to soothe overwrought nerves.

'*Scata! Scata!*' shouted the Captain. 'My spittle on "Never on Sunday"! I ask you for the cultural heritage of Greece and you give me a song about a "*poutana*". Is that culture? Is that necessary?'

'*Poutanas* are necessary for the crew,' the Chief Officer pointed out. 'For me, I'm a happily married man . . .'

'I don't want to know about *poutanas*,' snarled the Captain. 'Is there no one on this ship who can play any real Greek songs?'

'Well,' said the Chief Officer, 'there's the electrician, Taki, he has a bouzouki – and I think one of the engineers has a guitar.'

'Bring them!' roared the Captain. 'Bring everyone who can play Greek songs.'

'Suppose they *all* play ' said the Chief Officer, who was of a literal turn of mind. 'Who'd run the ship?'

'Get them, idiot,' snarled the Captain, and with such vehemence that the Chief Officer blanched and faded away.

Having shown his authority, the Captain's good humour returned. Beaming twinklingly, he returned to the table and ordered more drinks. Presently, from the bowels of the ship, struggled a motley gang, most of them half dressed, carrying between them three bouzoukis, a flute and two guitars. There was even a man with a harmonica. The Captain was delighted, but dismissed the man with the harmonica, to the poor man's obvious chagrin.

'But, Captain,' he protested, 'I play well.'

'It is not a Greek instrument,' said the Captain austerely. 'It is Italian. Do you think that when we built the Acropolis we went around playing Italian instruments?'

'But I play well,' the man persisted. 'I can play "Never on Sunday".'

Luckily the Purser hurried him out of the night-cloob before his Captain could get at him.

The rest of the evening went splendidly, with only minor accidents to mar the general air of cultural jollification. Leslie ricked his back while trying to leap in the air and slap his heels in the approved style during a strenuous *Hosapiko*, and Larry sprained his ankle by slipping on some melon pips that somebody had thoughtfully deposited on the dance floor. The same, but more painful, fate overtook the barman who, endeavouring to dance with what he thought was a glass of water on his head, slipped and crashed backwards. The glass tipped over his face. Unfortunately it did not contain water but ouzo – a liquid similar in appearance but more virulent in effect when splashed in your eyes. His sight was saved by the presence of mind of the Purser who seized a siphon of soda and directed into each eye of the unfortunate barman, a jet of such strength that it almost undid its therapeutic work by blowing out his eyeballs. He was led off to his cabin, moaning, and the dance continued. The dance went on until dawn, when, like a candle, it dwindled and flickered and went out. We crept tiredly to our beds as the sky was turning from opal to blue and the sea was striped with scarves of mist.

All was bustle and activity when we dragged ourselves out of bed and assembled, as we had been told, in the main saloon.

Presently, the Purser materialized, and bowed to Mother and Margo. The Captain's compliments, he said, and would we all like to go on to the bridge and see the ship dock? Mother consented to attend this great moment with such graciousness that you would have thought that they had asked her to launch the ship. After a hurried and typical Greek breakfast (cold toast, cold bacon and eggs, served on iced plates, accompanied by lukewarm tea which turned out to be coffee in a teapot for some mysterious reason), we trooped up on to the bridge.

The Captain, looking slightly jowly but with no loss of charm after his hard night, greeted us with great joy, presented Mother and Margo with carnations, showed us round the wheelhouse with pride, and then took us out on what Larry insisted on calling the quarter-deck. From here, we had a perfect view over both the bows and the stern of the vessel. The Chief Officer stood by the winch round which the anchor chain was coiled like a strange rusty necklace, and near him stood at least three of the sailors who had made up last night's band. They all waved and blew kisses to Margo.

'Margo, dear, I do wish you wouldn't be so familiar with those sailors,' complained Mother.

'Oh, Mother, don't be so old-fashioned,' said Margo, blowing lavish kisses back. 'After all, I've got an ex-husband and two children.'

'It's by blowing kisses at strange sailors that you get ex-husbands and children,' remarked Mother, grimly.

'Now,' said the Captain, his teeth glittering in the sun, 'you come, Miss Margo, and I show you our radar. Radar so we can avoid rocks, collisions, catastrophes at sea. If Ulysses had had this, he would have travelled farther, eh? Beyond the portals of Hercules, eh? Then we Greeks would have discovered America . . . Come.'

He led Margo into the wheelhouse and was busily showing her the radar. The ship was now pointing straight at the docks, travelling at the speed of an elderly man on a bicycle. The Chief

63

Officer, his eyes fixed on the bridge like a retriever poised to fetch in the first grouse of the season, waited anxiously for instructions. Inside the bridge-house, the Captain was explaining to Margo how, with radar, the Greeks could have discovered Australia, as well as America. Leslie began to get worried, for we were now quite close to the docks.

'I say, Captain,' he called. 'Shouldn't we drop anchor?'

The Captain turned from beaming into Margo's face and fixed Leslie with a frigid stare.

'Please not to worry, Mr Durrell,' he said. 'Everything is under control.'

Then he turned and saw the dock looming ahead like an implacable cement iceberg.

'Mother of God help me!' he roared in Greek, and bounded out of the wheelhouse.

'Papadopoulos!' he screamed. 'Let go the anchor!'

This was the signal the Chief Officer had been waiting for. There was a burst of activity, and a roar and clatter as the chain was pulled by the heavy anchor, the splash as the anchor hit the sea, and the rattle as the chain continued running out. The ship went inexorably on its way. More and more chain rattled out, and still the ship slid on. It was obvious that the anchor had been released too late to act in its normal capacity as a brake. The Captain, ready for any emergency as a good Captain should be, leapt into the wheelhouse, signalled full astern, and brought the wheel hard over, pushing the helmsman out of the way with great violence. Alas, his brilliant summation of the situation, his rapid thinking, his magnificent manoeuvre, could not save us.

With her bow still swinging round, the *Poseidon* hit the docks with a tremendous crash. At the speed we were travelling, I thought that we would only feel the merest shudder. I was wrong. It felt as though we had struck a mine. The entire family fell in a heap. The three fat ladies, who had been descending a companionway, were flung down it like an avalanche

64

of bolsters. In fact, everyone, including the Captain, fell down. Larry received a nasty cut on the forehead, Mother bruised her ribs, Margo only laddered her stockings. The Captain with great agility, regained his feet, did various technical things at the wheel, signalled the engine room, and then – his face black with rage – strode out on to the bridge.

'Papadopoulos!' he roared at the poor Chief Officer, who was getting shakily to his feet and mopping blood from his nose, 'you son of a *poutana*, you imbecile, you donkey! You illegitimate son of a ditch-delivered Turkish cretin! Why didn't you lower the anchor?'

'But Captain,' began the Chief Officer, his voice muffled behind a blood-stained handkerchief, 'you never told me to.'

'Am I expected to do everything around here,' bellowed the Captain. 'Steer the ship, run the engines, produce the band which can play the Greek songs? Mother of God!' He clapped his face in his hands.

All around arose the cacophony of Greeks in a SITUATION. With this noise, and the Captain's tragic figure, it seemed rather like a scene from the battle of Trafalgar.

'Well,' said Larry, mopping blood from his eyes, 'this *was* a splendid idea, Mother. I do congratulate you. I think, however, I will fly back. That is, *if* we can get ashore alive.'

Eventually, the walking wounded were allowed ashore and we straggled down the gangway. We could now see that the *Poseidon* had another, almost identical, hole in her bows, on the opposite side to the previous one.

'Well, at least now she matches,' said Leslie gloomily.

'Oh, look!' said Margo, as we stood on the docks. 'There's that poor old band.'

She waved, and the three old gentlemen bowed. We saw that the violinist had a nasty cut on his forehead and the tuba player a piece of sticking-plaster across the bridge of his nose. They returned our bows and, obviously interpreting the appearance of the family as a sign of support that would do something to restore their sense of dignity which had been so sorely undermined by their ignominious dismissal of the night before, they turned in unison, glanced up at the bridge, with looks of great defiance raised tuba, trombone and violin, and started to play.

The strains of 'Never on Sunday' floated down to us.

THE PUBLIC SCHOOL
EDUCATION

Venice is one of the most beautiful of European cities and one
that I had visited frequently but never stayed in. I had always
been on my way to somewhere else and so had never had the
time for proper exploration. So, one red-hot summer when I
had been working hard and was feeling tired and in need of a
change, I decided that I would go and spend a week in Venice
and relax and get to know her. I felt that a calming holiday in
such a setting was exactly what I needed. I have rarely regretted a decision more; if I had known what was going to
happen to me I would have fled to New York or Buenos
Aires or Singapore rather than set foot in that most elegant of
cities.

I drove through the beautiful and incomparable France,
through orderly Switzerland, over the high passes where there
were still ugly piles of dirty grey snow at the edge of the roads
and then down into Italy and towards my destination. The
weather remained perfect until I reached the causeway that
leads into Venice. Here the sky, with miraculous suddenness,
turned from blue to black, became veined with fern-like threads
of intense blue and white lightning, and then disgorged a
torrent of rain of such magnitude that it made windscreen

wipers futile and brought a great chain of traffic to a standstill. Hundreds of hysterically twitching Italians sat there, nose to tail, immobilized by the downpour, trying to ease their frustration by blowing their horns cacophonously, and screaming abuse at each other above the roar of the rain.

At length, edging forward inch by inch I finally managed to get the car to the garage at the end of the causeway. Having successfully berthed her, I found myself a burly porter to carry my bags. At a run we galloped through the teeming rain to the docks where the speedboat belonging to the hotel into which I had booked lay waiting. My suitcases were drenched with rain, and by the time they had been put on board the boat, and I had tipped the porter and got on board myself, my thin tropical suit was a limp, damp rag. The moment, however, that the speedboat started up the rain died down to a very fine, drifting mizzle which hung across the canals like a fine veil of lawn, muting the russets and browns and pinks of the buildings so that they looked like a beautifully faded Canaletto painting.

We sped down the Grand Canal and when we reached my hotel the boat put into the hotel jetty. As the engine stuttered and died we were passed by a gondola, propelled in a rather disconsolate fashion by a very damp-looking gondolier. The two people occupying it were shielded from the inclemencies of the weather by a large umbrella and so I could not see their faces, but, as the gondola passed us and sped down a narrow side canal that led to Marco Polo's house, I heard a penetrating female English voice (obviously the product of Roedean, that most expensive of public schools), float out from under the umbrella.

'Of course, Naples is just like Venice only without so much water,' it observed in flute-like tones.

I stood riveted on the landing stage outside the hotel, staring after the retreating gondola. Surely, I said to myself, I must be dreaming, and yet in my experience there was only one voice in the world like that; only one voice, moreover, capable of making such a ridiculous statement. It belonged to a girl-friend of mine whom I had not seen for some thirty years, Ursula Pendragon-White. She, of all my girl-friends, I think I adored the most, but she was also the one who filled me with the most alarm and despondency.

It was not only her command over the English language that caused me pain (it was she who had told me about a friend of hers who had had an ablution so she would not have an il-legitimate baby), but her interference in the private lives of her wide circle of acquaintances. When I had last known her she was busy trying to reform a friend of hers who, she said, was drinking so much that he was in danger of becoming an in-coherent.

But no, I thought to myself, it could not be Ursula. She was safely and happily married to a very dull young man and lived in the depths of Hampshire. What on earth would she be doing in Venice at a time of year when all good farmer's wives were helping their husbands get the harvest in, or organizing jumble sales in the village. In any case, I thought to myself, even if it *was* Ursula I did not want to get tangled up with her again. I had come here for peace and quiet, and from my past experience of her I knew that close contact with her brought anything but that. Speaking as one who had had to pursue a Pekinese puppy through a crowded theatre during a Mozart concert, I knew that Ursula could get one involved in the most horrifying of predicaments without even really trying. No, no, I thought, it could not have been Ursula, and even if it *had* been thank God she had not spotted me.

The hotel was sumptuous and my large and ornate bedroom overlooking the Grand Canal was exceedingly comfortable. After I had changed out of my wet things and had a bath and a drink I saw that the weather had changed and the sun was blazing, making the whole of Venice glitter in a delicate sunset of colours. I walked down numerous little alleyways, crossed tiny bridges over canals, until I came at length to the vast

Piazza San Marco, lined with bars, each of which had its own orchestra. Hundreds of pigeons wheeled and swooped through the brilliant air as people purchased bags of corn and scattered this largess for the birds on to the mosaic of the huge square. I picked my way through the sea of birds until I reached the Doge's Palace where there was a collection of pictures that I wanted to see. The Palace was crammed with hundreds of sight-seers of a dozen different nationalities, from Japanese, festooned like Christmas trees with cameras, to portly, guttural Germans and lithe blond Swedes. Wedged in this human lava flow I progressed slowly from room to room, admiring the paintings. Suddenly I heard the penetrating flute-like voice up ahead of me in the crowd.

'Last year, in Spain,' it said, 'I went to see all those pictures by Gruyère . . . so gloomy, with lots of corpses and things. So depressing, not like these. I really do think that Cannelloni is positively my favourite Italian painter. Scrumptious!'

Now I knew, beyond a shadow of doubt, that it was Ursula. No other woman would be capable of getting a cheese, a pasta and two painters so inextricably entwined. I shifted cautiously through the crowd until I could see her distinctive profile, the large brilliant blue eyes, the long tip-tilted nose, the end of which looked as if it had been snipped off – an enchanting effect – and her cloud-like mass of hair still, to my surprise, dark, but with streaks of silver in it. She looked as lovely as ever and the years had dealt kindly with her.

She was with a middle-aged, very bewildered-looking man, who was gazing at her in astonishment at her culinary-artistic observation. I felt, from his amazement that he must be a comparatively new acquaintance, for anyone who had known Ursula for any length of time would take her last statement in his stride.

Beautiful and enchanting though she was, I felt it would be safer for my peace of mind not to renew my acquaintance with her lest something diabolical resulted to ruin my holiday.

Reluctantly, I left the Palace, determined to come back the following day when I felt Ursula would have had her fill of pictures. I made my way back into the Piazza San Marco, found a pleasant café and sat down to a well-earned brandy and soda. All the cafés around the square were packed with people and in such a crowd I was, I felt, certain to escape observation. In any case I was sure Ursula would not recognize me, for I was several stone heavier than when she had last seen me, my hair was grey and I now sported a beard.

Feeling safe, I sat there to enjoy my drink and listen to the charming Strauss waltzes the band was playing. The sunshine, my pleasant drink and the soothing music lulled me into a sense of false security. I had forgotten Ursula's ability – a sense well developed in most women but in her case enlarged to magical proportion – to walk into a crowded room, take one glance around in a casual way and then be able to tell you, not only who was in the room but what they were all wearing. So I shouldn't have felt the shock and surprise I did when I suddenly heard her scream above the chatter of the crowd and the noise of the band.

'Darling, darling,' she cried, hurrying through the tables towards me. 'Darling Gerry, it's *me*, Ursula!'

I rose to meet my fate. Ursula rushed into my arms, fastened her mouth on mine and gave me a prolonged kiss accompanied by humming noises, of the sort that (even in this permissive day and age) were of the variety which one generally reserved for the bedroom. Presently, when I began to think that we might be arrested by the Italian police for disorderly behaviour, Ursula dragged her mouth reluctantly away from mine and stood back, holding tightly on to my hands.

'Darling,' she cooed, her huge blue eyes brimming with tears of delight, '*darling* . . . I can't *believe* it . . . seeing you again after all these *years* . . . it's a miracle . . . oh, I am so happy, darling. How scrumptious to see you again.'

'How did you know it was me?' I asked feebly.

'How did I know, darling? You *are* silly . . . you haven't changed a *bit*,' she said untruthfully. 'Besides, darling, I've seen you on television and your photos on the covers of your books, so naturally I would recognize you.'

'Well, it's very nice to see you again,' I went on guardedly.

'Darling, it's been simply an *age*,' she said, '*far* too long.' She had, I noticed, divested herself of the bewildered-looking gentleman.

'Sit down and have a drink,' I suggested.

'Of course, sweetie, I'd *love* one.' She seated herself, willowy and elegant, at my table. I beckoned the waiter.

'What are you drinking?' she asked.

'Brandy and soda.'

'Ugh!' she cried, shuddering delicately. 'How positively *revolting*. You shouldn't drink it, darling, you'll end up with halitosis of the liver.'

'Never mind my liver,' I said, long-sufferingly. 'What do you want to drink?'

'I'll have one of those Bonny Prince Charlie things.'

The waiter stared at her blankly. He did not have the benefit of my early training with Ursula.

'Madam would like a Dubonnet,' I said, 'and I'll have another brandy.'

I sat down at the table and Ursula leant forward, gave me a ravishing, melting smile and seized my hand in both of hers.

'Darling, isn't this *romantic*?' she asked. 'You and me meeting after all these years in *Venice*? It's the most romantic thing I've heard of, don't you think?'

'Yes,' I said cautiously, 'how's your husband?'

'Oh, didn't you know? I'm divorced.'

'I'm sorry.'

'Oh, it's all right,' she explained. 'It was better really. You see, poor dear, he was never the same after he got foot and mouth disease.'

Even my previous experience of Ursula had not prepared me for this.

'Toby got foot and mouth disease?' I asked.

'Yes . . . *terribly*,' she said with a sigh, 'and he was never really the same again.'

'I should think not. But surely cases of humans getting it must be very rare?'

'Humans?' she said, wide-eyed. 'What d'you mean?'

'Well, you said that Toby . . .' I began, when Ursula gave a shriek of laughter.

'You are *silly*,' she crowed. 'I meant that all his *cattle* got it. His whole pedigree herd that had taken him *years* to breed. He had to kill the lot, and it seemed to affect him a lot, poor lamb. He started going about with the most curious women and getting drunk in night clubs and that sort of thing.'

'I never realized that foot and mouth disease could have such far-reaching effects,' I said. 'I wonder if the Ministry of Agriculture knows?'

'D'you think they'd be *interested*?' Ursula asked in astonishment. 'I could write to them about it if you thought I ought to.'

'No, no,' I said, hastily, 'I was only joking.'

'Well,' she said, 'tell me about your marriage.'

'I'm divorced, too,' I confessed.

'You *are*? Darling, I told you this meeting was romantic,' she said misty-eyed. 'The two of us meeting in Venice with broken marriages. It's just like a *book*, darling.'

'Well, I don't think we ought to read too much into it.'

'What are you doing in Venice?' she asked.

'Nothing,' I said, unguardedly. 'I'm just here for a holiday.'

'Oh, wonderful, darling, then you can help me,' she exclaimed.

'*No!*' I said hastily, 'I won't help you.'

'Darling, you don't even know what I'm asking you to *do*,' she said plaintively.

'I don't care *what* it is, I'm not doing it.'

'Sweetie, this is the first time we've met in *ages* and you're being horrid to me before we even start,' she said indignantly.

'I don't care. I know all about your machinations from bitter experience and I do not intend to spend my holiday getting mixed up with whatever awful things you are doing.'

'You're *beastly*,' she said, her eyes brimming, blue as flax flowers, her red mouth quivering. 'You're perfectly *beastly* . . . here am I alone in Venice, without a husband, and you won't lift a finger to help me in my distress. You're *revolting* and *unchivalrous* . . . and . . . *beastly*.'

I groaned. 'Oh, all right, all right, tell me about it. But I warn you I'm not getting involved. I came here for peace and quiet.'

'Well,' said Ursula, drying her eyes and taking a sip of her drink, 'I'm here on what you might call an errand of mercy. The whole thing is fraught with difficulty and imprecations.'

'Imprecations?' I asked, fascinated in spite of myself.

Ursula looked around to make sure we were alone. As we were only surrounded by some five thousand junketing foreigners she felt it was safe to confide in me.

'Imprecations in high places,' she said, lowering her voice. 'It's something you must not let go any further.'

'Don't you mean implications?' I asked, wanting to get the whole thing on to a more or less intelligible plane.

'I mean what I say,' said Ursula frostily. 'I do wish you'd stop trying to correct me. It was one of your worst characteristics in the old days that you would go on and *on* correcting me. It's very irritating, darling.'

'I'm sorry,' I said contritely, 'do go on and tell me who in high places is imprecating whom.'

'Well,' she said, lowering her voice to such an extent that I could hardly hear her in the babble of noise that surrounded us, 'it involves the Duke of Tolpuddle. That's why I've had to come to Venice because *I'm* the only one Reggie and Marjorie will trust and Perry, too, for that matter, and of course the Duke who is an absolute *sweetie* and is naturally so cut up about the whole thing, what with the scandal and everything, and so naturally when I said I'd come they jumped at it. But you mustn't say a word about it to *anyone*, darling, promise?'

'What am I not to say a word about?' I asked, dazedly, signalling the waiter for more drinks.

'But I've just told you,' said Ursula impatiently. 'About Reggie and Marjorie and Perry. And, of course, the Duke.'

I took a deep breath: 'But I don't *know* Reggie and Marjorie and Perry *or* the Duke.'

'You don't?' asked Ursula, amazed.

I remembered then that she was always astonished to find that you did not know everyone in her wide circle of incredibly dull acquaintances.

'No. So, as you will see, it is difficult for me to understand the problem. As far as I am aware, it may range from them all having developed leprosy to the Duke being caught operating an illicit still.'

'Don't be silly, darling,' said Ursula, shocked. 'There's no insanity in the family.'

I sighed. 'Look, just tell me who did what to whom, remembering that I don't *know* any of them, and I have a feeling that I don't want to.'

'Well,' said Ursula, 'Peregrine is the Duke's only son. He's just eighteen and a really nice boy, in spite of it.'

'In spite of what?' I asked, muddled.

'Adulteration,' said Ursula, ominously and incomprehensibly.

I decided not to try to disentangle this one.

'Go on,' I said, hoping that things would become clearer.

'Well, Perry was at St Jonah's . . . you know, that frightfully posh school that they say is better than Eton or Harrow?'

'The one that costs ten thousand pounds a term without food? Yes, I've heard of it.'

'My dear, only the *very best* people's children get sent there,' said Ursula, 'it's as exclusive as . . . as . . . as . . .'

'Harrods?'

'Well, more or less,' agreed Ursula, doubtfully.

'So Perry was at St Jonah's,' I prompted.

'Yes, and doing *frightfully* well, so the headmaster said. And out of the blue came this bolt,' she said, lowering her voice to a penetrating whisper.

'Bolt?' I said, puzzled. 'What bolt?'

'Out of the blue, darling,' went on Ursula impatiently, 'You know how bolts come. I do wish you'd stop interrupting, darling and let me get on with the story.'

'I wish you'd get on with the story, too,' I said. 'So far all I've got out of it is an adulterated Duke's son with a bolt, and I have no means of knowing whether this is an affliction or not.'

'Well, be quiet and let me *tell* you. If you'd stop talking for a moment I could get a word in sideways.'

I sighed.

'All right,' I said, 'I'll be quiet.'

'Thank you, darling,' said Ursula, squeezing my hand. 'Well, as I say, Perry was doing frightfully well when along came this bolt. Reggie and Marjorie went to the school. Reggie was employed as their art master because, you know, he is awfully good at oil-painting and etching and things like that, although I do think he's rather eccentric and so I was surprised at St Jonah's taking him, really, because it's so posh that they don't really go in for eccentrics, if you know what I mean?'

'Why is he eccentric?'

'Well, my dear, don't *you* think it's eccentric to have an oil-painting of your wife *in the nude* hung over the mantelpiece in your *drawing-room*? I told him I thought it was more suitable for the bathroom, if you *had* to put it on the wall, and he said that he had thought of hanging it in the guest bedroom. I ask you, darling, if *that's* not eccentric, what is?'

I did not say so, but I rather warmed to Reggie.

'So Reggie was the bolt?' I enquired.

'No, darling, *Marjorie* was the bolt. The moment Perry saw her he fell violently in love with her, because she *is* rather beautiful – if you like those women from the South Seas that Chopin used to paint.'

'Gauguin?' I suggested.

'Probably,' said Ursula vaguely. 'Anyway, she really is quite pretty, but I think she's just a weeny bit stupid. Well, she behaved very stupidly with Perry because she encouraged him. And then came another bolt.'

'Another bolt?' I queried, steeling myself.

'Yes,' she said. 'My dear, the silly girl went and fell in love with Perry, and as you know she's almost old enough to be his mother *and* has a baby. Well, perhaps she's not old enough to be his *mother*, exactly, but he's eighteen and she's thirty if she's a day, although she always swears she's twenty-six, but anyway, it doesn't alter the fact that the whole thing was most unsuitable. Naturally, Reggie got very despondent.'

'He could have solved the problem by giving Perry the portrait of Marjorie,' I suggested.

Ursula gave me a reproving look.

'It's no laughing matter, darling,' she said severely. 'We have all been in a complete turmoil, I can tell you.'

I was fascinated by the thought of seeing a Duke in a turmoil, but I did not say so.

'So what happened?' I asked.

'Well, Reggie tackled Marjorie and she confessed that she had fallen in love with Perry and that they had been having an affair behind the gym, of all uncomfortable places. So, not unnaturally, Reggie got fearfully annoyed and gave her a black eye, which was really quite uncalled for, as I told him. He then went looking for Perry to give *him* a black eye, I suppose, but luckily Perry had gone home for the week-end, so Reggie couldn't find him, which was just as well because Perry's not a very strong boy, poor dear, whereas Reggie is built like an *ox*, as well as having a terrible temper.'

Now that the plot had started to unfold, I found myself starting to take an interest in it, in spite of myself.

'Go on,' I said, 'what happened next?'

'This is the worst part of the whole thing,' said Ursula, in her penetrating whisper. She took a sip of her drink and glanced around to make sure that the whole of Venice, now assembled around us for a pre-lunchtime drink, was not eavesdropping. She leant forward and pulled me towards her by my hand. I leant across the table and she whispered in my ear. 'They eloped,' she hissed, and sat back to see the effect of her words.

'You mean Reggie and Perry eloped?' I asked, in well-simulated astonishment.

'Idiot,' said Ursula angrily, 'you know *perfectly* well what I mean, Perry and Marjorie eloped. I do wish you would stop making fun of this, it's *very* serious.'

'I'm sorry,' I said, 'do go on.'

'Well,' said Ursula, slightly mollified by my apology, 'of course this really put a cat among the pigeons. Reggie was simply furious because Marjorie had not only eloped but had taken the baby and the nannie with her.'

'It certainly sounds like a very overcrowded elopement.'

'And naturally,' Ursula continued, 'Perry's father took it very hard. As you can imagine it's difficult for a Duke to condone his only son's adulteration.'

'But adultery is when the husband is at fault, as a rule,' I protested.

'I don't care *who*'s at fault,' said Ursula firmly, 'it's still adulteration.'

I sighed. The problem itself seemed complex enough without the additional difficulty of having Ursula's interpretation of it.

'In any case,' she went on, 'as I told Marjorie it was as good as incest.'

78

'*Incest?*'

'Yes,' said Ursula, 'after all the boy was under age and in any case, as she well knew, adulteration has to be done by adults.'

I took a deep drink of my brandy to steady myself. It was obvious that Ursula had grown worse over the years.

'I think I had better take you to lunch while you tell me the rest of this.'

'Oh, darling, *will* you? How wonderful. But I mustn't be late because I've got to go to Marjorie's, because I don't know where Reggie is and the Duke's arriving.'

'You mean,' I said slowly and carefully, 'that all these people you have been talking about are *here*, in Venice?'

'But *of course*, sweetie,' she said, wide-eyed. 'That's why I want you to *help* me. Didn't you *understand?*'

'No,' I said, 'I didn't understand. But just remember that I have not the slightest intention of getting muddled up in this affair. Let's go and have lunch . . . where would you like to go?'

'I'd like to go to the "Laughing Cat",' said Ursula.

'Where the hell's that?'

'I don't know, but I was told it was very good,' she said, powdering her nose.

'All right, I'll find out,' I said. I called the waiter over, paid for the drinks and asked the way to the "Laughing Cat". It turned out to be within easy walking distance of the Piazza San Marco, a small but well-appointed little restaurant which, judging by the fact that most of its clientele were Venetians, was going to provide us with pretty substantial fare. We found a pleasant table out on the pavement under an awning, and I ordered mussels simmered in cream and parsley, followed by stuffed shoulder of kid with a chestnut purée the way they serve it in Corsica. We were – fortunately – just demolishing the kid (which melted in your mouth), and were thinking in terms of some Dolcelatte cheese to be followed, perhaps, by some fresh fruit, when Ursula, looking over my shoulder, gave a gasp of horror. I looked round to see a very powerful, and exceedingly drunk gentleman approaching our table, tacking from side to side like a yacht.

'Oh, my God, it's Reggie,' said Ursula. 'How did he know they were in Venice?'

'It's all right, they're not *here*,' I pointed out.

'But they will be in a minute,' wailed Ursula. 'I've arranged to meet them and the Duke here. What shall I do? Quick, darling, think of something.'

Whether I liked it or not it seemed inevitable that I was going to get embroiled in this whole ridiculous saga. I took a deep draught of wine to steady myself and rose to my feet as Reggie, more by good luck than good management, arrived at our table.

'Reggie, darling,' cried Ursula, 'what a *lovely* surprise. What are you doing in Venice?'

' 'Lo, Ursula,' said Reggie, swaying gently and having difficulty in focusing his eyes and enunciating with clarity, 'amin Ven . . . Vennish to kill a dirty rat . . . a dirty loushy little rat, thass what I'm in Vennish for . . . thass what, see?'

Not only was Reggie a large man, built on the lines of an all-in wrestler, but he had a large pithecanthropic face with a straggling beard and moustache. He was partly bald and wore his hair at shoulder length. To add to this singularly unattractive appearance he was wearing a bright ginger, ill-fitting tweed suit, a scarlet roll-top pullover and sandals. Nevertheless, he did look quite capable of killing young Perry if he could get hold of him, and I began to give serious thought to the problem of luring him out of the restaurant before the other protagonists arrived.

'Reggie, darling, this is a friend of mine, Gerry Durrell,' said Ursula, breathlessly.

'Pleeshtermeetyer,' said Reggie, holding out a hand like a Bayonne ham and wringing mine in a vice-like grip.

'Do join us for a drink?' I suggested and Ursula gave me a warning look. I winked at her.

'Drink,' said Reggie throatily, leaning heavily on the table. 'Thash what I want . . . a drink . . . sheveral *big* drinks . . . all in a big glash . . . hunereds and hunereds of drinks . . . I'll have a double whishky and water.'

I got him a chair and he sat down heavily. I beckoned the waiter and ordered whisky.

'Do you think you ought to drink any more?' asked Ursula, unwisely. 'It seems to me you've had rather a lot already, darling.'

'Are you surghesting I'm drunk?' asked Reggie ominously.

'No, no,' said Ursula, hastily, realizing her error. 'I just thought perhaps another drink wouldn't be a very good idea.'

'I,' said Reggie, pointing a finger the size of a banana at his chest so that we should be in no doubt as to whom he was referring, 'I'm as jober as a sudge.'

The waiter arrived with the drink and placed it in front of Reggie.

'Drink, thash what *I* want,' said Reggie, lifting the glass somewhat unsteadily. 'Here's death to all miser . . . miserub-bubble creeping little arish . . . arishtocratic pimps.'

He drained the glass and sat back with a look of satisfaction on his face. 'Lesh have another one,' he suggested cheerfully.

'Why don't we toddle along to the Piazza San Marco and have another drink there?' I suggested smoothly.

'Ooo, yes, what a good idea,' chimed in Ursula.

'I'm not narrow minded,' said Reggie earnestly. 'I don' mind *where* I drink.'

'Right, San Marco it is,' I decided, beckoning the waiter for the bill.

Before he could bring it, however, we were (as Ursula would, no doubt, have put it) hit by a bolt from the blue. I heard her give a despairing squeak of alarm, and turned to find a tall, thin, rather aristocratic gentleman at my elbow, who looked not unlike a grey praying mantis in a Savile Row suit and shoes that had obviously been made for him at Lobb's. In addition he was wearing an old Etonian tie, and had a triangle of Irish linen handkerchief, the size of a rabbit's scut, peeping out of his breast pocket. He had silver grey hair, a silver grey face and a silver grey monocle in one silver grey eye. This, I decided, could only be the Duke of Tolpuddle.

'Ursula, my dear child, I *am* so sorry to be late, but my wretched vaporetto broke down. I *do* apologize,' he said, beaming at Reggie and me, exuding well-bred charm, secure in the knowledge that, with the blue blood that flowed in his veins, he would always be sure of a welcome, however late he was.

'Oh, oh . . . er . . . oh, don't mention it,' said Ursula faintly.

'And who are your friends?' asked the Duke, benignly, ready to treat Reggie and I as if we were members of the human race. I realized, with delicious satisfaction, that the Duke and Reggie did not know each other. I sat back and beamed at Ursula, who gave me a despairing look out of her huge, hunted blue eyes.

'Do introduce us, darling,' I said.

Ursula glared at me.

'Well,' she said at length, 'this is an old friend of mine, Gerry Durrell and this is . . . and this is . . . er . . . this is Reggie Montrose.'

The Duke stiffened, and his benign expression slipped for a brief moment. Then he straightened up and screwed his monocle more firmly into his eyes, preparing himself to do the decent thing.

'Whoes thish?' enquired Reggie, focusing the Duke with difficulty.

Ursula looked at me desperately. I shrugged. There was, after all, nothing I could do to fend off the crisis.

'Whoes *thish* blighter?' asked Reggie, pointing a banana finger at the Duke.

'This is . . . er . . . this is . . . er . . . the Duke of Tolpuddle,' said Ursula in a small voice.

It took a moment or so for the news to sink into Reggie's brain cells through the layers of alcohol, but it got there eventually.

'Tolpuzzle? Tolpuzzle?' he said. 'D'you meantershay thish ish the father of that little bashtard?'

'I say,' said the Duke, looking about the restaurant in the furtive fashion of an English gentleman, hating any sort of altercation in public. 'I say, old man, steady on, what? No cause for that sort of language in front of ladies.'

Reggie rose slowly and unsteadily to his feet and waggled an enormous finger under the Duke's aquiline nose.

'Don' you tell *me* what language to use,' he said belligerently. 'Don' you go giving *me* advish! Why don' you go and give advish to that little bashtard fart you shired, if indeed you did *shire* him, becaushe from where I'm shtanding, you don' look ash if you could shire a mentally retarded Chihuahua.'

To my relief he sat down again, rather heavily, and for a moment I thought he was going to topple the chair over backwards. With an effort he managed to right it. The Duke had gone a dull red. It must have been irritating to know that Reggie, however badly behaved, was after all the plaintiff and that his son was the guilty party.

'I think,' said the Duke, bringing to bear the centuries of aristocratic breeding that was his birthright, 'I think we ought to sit down and talk about this in a civilized manner, and not descend to vulgar abuse.'

'Frog's ovaries,' said Reggie, loudly and clearly.

'Reggie, darling, please behave,' said Ursula.

'Who?' asked Reggie, as earnestly as one seeking knowledge from a sage, 'who does this old fart think he ish, eh?'

'Do sit down and join us, sir,' I said heartily.

Ursula gave me a look that would – if I had not been enjoying myself so much – have withered me root and branch.

'Thank you,' said the Duke, icily, 'but there does not seem to be a chair, and your friend is making it more than apparent that I am, to say the least, *de trop*.'

'I'll get a chair for you,' I said hospitably, and beckoned the waiter. A chair being procured the Duke sat down rather gingerly, as if expecting it to give way under his weight.

'Would you care for a drink, sir?' I asked, playing the anxious host.

'Drinks,' said Reggie with satisfaction, 'lots of bloody great drinks . . . gallons and gallons of butts of malmsey . . . you can't dink without trinking.'

'Thank you, I will have a small, dry sherry, if I may,' said the Duke.

'That little bashtard of yours doesn't drink,' said Reggie, 'all he takes is Coca-Cola and mother's milk . . . he is an invert . . . an invert . . . an invertebrate if ever I shaw one . . . tototally and completely shpineless.'

'Now look here, Mr Montrose,' said the Duke, tried beyond endurance, tapping his beautifully manicured fingers on the table, 'I have no wish to quarrel with you. My reason for being in Venice should not strike you as inimical to your own affairs. If you will just allow me to explain, I think I can clarify the situation and, to some extent, put your mind at ease.'

'The only way you can put my mind at eash is to get your bloody little son out of my wife's bed,' said Reggie, loudly and belligerently.

The Duke threw an embarrassed look round the restaurant. All the Italians, not being used to such uninhibited displays from Anglo-Saxons (particularly the British) were watching us with lively curiosity.

'I have come to Venice to try to do precisely that,' said the Duke.

'What you gonna do?' asked Reggie. 'Get him shom one elshes wife?'

'I propose to deal with him very firmly,' said the Duke. 'I dislike this liaison as much, if not more, than you do and it must end.'

'Don' you refer to my wife as a lia . . . lia . . . liaison,' said Reggie, going a shade of angry purple that threatened imminence of cardiac arrest. 'Who t'hell d'you think you are, referring to my wife as a liaison, eh?'

'I meant no disrespect,' said the Duke coldly, 'but I am sure you will agree that the whole thing is most unsuitable. I will say nothing about the disparity of their ages. That in itself is appalling. But looking beyond that you must realize that the boy is after all, heir to the title and so it behoves him to be careful about whom he associates with.'

Reggie stared at him for a long moment.

'You are without doubt the biggest piesch of per . . . perambulating horse shit it has ever been my misfortune to encounter,' he said at length.

'Reggie, darling, you can't say things like that to the *Duke*,' put in Ursula, shocked.

'Why not?' asked Reggie reasonably. 'If he thinks my wife's unshutable for that puke of a son of his then I shay he is indub . . . indub . . . undoubtably the biggest and smelliest piece of perambulating horse shit this side of Ascot.'

He and the Duke glared at each other. It was at that precise moment that Ursula uttered another piercing squeak and we were hit by the second bolt from the blue. Perry and Marjorie, hand in hand, entered the restaurant. Marjorie was a handsome lady who did look a little like a Gauguin maiden, and Perry was a willowy, delicate, and rather beautiful young man in the Byronic style. I had just time to register this before Reggie, uttering a noise like a dyspeptic lion with a thorn in its paw, rose to his feet and pointed a quivering finger at the happy couple, who had become rooted to the spot with horror at being so suddenly confronted.

'There's the little puke and his liaison,' shouted Reggie. 'Well, I tell you what I'm going to do . . .'

Unwisely, as it turned out, I got to my feet and laid a restraining hand on Reggie's shoulder.

85

'Now hang on, Reggie,' I said soothingly. 'You're three times his size and . . .'

I got no further. Gathering my coat into a bunch in one enormous hand, Reggie picked me up as though I had been a piece of thistledown and deposited me with care and accuracy on a sweet trolley that a waiter happened to be conveniently wheeling past. My contact with it did irreparable damage to several pêches melba, a very fine strawberry tart, a delicious-looking trifle of singularly clinging consistency, and a great number of different species of ice cream. Perry, at the sight of this display of violence, came out of his trance. Letting go of Marjorie's hand, he turned and fled with the utmost speed. Uttering another lion-like roar Reggie, showing agility astonishing in one of his build, ran after him. He, in turn, was pursued by Marjorie shouting, 'Murderer, don't you dare touch him,' and by the Duke, who was calling, 'Harm a hair of his head and I'll sue you!' Dripping ice cream, trifle and strawberries in equal quantities, I did the only thing possible: I flung a huge handful of notes on to the table and, seizing Ursula's hand, ran after everyone.

As it turned out Perry had, rather unwisely, taken the little alleyway that led to the Piazza San Marco. If he had stuck to the alleyways he would have stood a chance of shaking off the pursuit but as it was, once he was out and running through flocks of frightened pigeons in the vast square, Reggie's superior turn of speed proved his undoing. Just as he reached the far side of the square, along which runs the Grand Canal, Reggie caught him by the scruff of the neck. The rest of us arrived in a panting mass, to find Reggie shaking Perry to and fro like a puppet, and shouting incoherently at him. I felt that I should intervene in some way but having already had proof that Reggie did not take kindly to interference, and with the Grand Canal at his elbow, I felt I owed it to myself to be a coward.

'Leave him alone, you gross bully,' shouted the Duke, between gasps for breath.

'Leave him alone, leave him alone, he's not strong,' shrilled Marjorie, beating the flat of her hands futilely on her husband's broad back.

'Darling, this is all *your* fault,' said Ursula, turning on me like a tigress. '*You* do something.'

Before I could protest at her perfidy, however, Reggie pulled Perry up close to him and glowered into his face.

'I'm shick of your bloody puke of a father and I'm shick of *you*,' he roared. 'So your bloody father doesn't think my wife's good enough for you, eh? eh? eh? Well, I'll show you! I'll divorce and then you can bloody well marry her.'

The Piazza San Marco is always a place of interest to tourists visiting Venice and so, not unnaturally, we now had a crowd of some five thousand people, of different colours and creeds, gathered around us expectant and interested.

'What did you s-s-s-say . . .?' asked Perry, white-faced, still being shaken to and fro in Reggie's massive grasp.

'I'll divorce my wife and then you can bloody well marry her,' Reggie roared.

'*Bravo! Quelle diplomatie*,' said a Frenchman in the crowd.

'You can rely on my son to do the proper thing,' declared the Duke, recovering from his shock at Reggie's announcement. 'After all, he had a public school education and so knows how to behave like a gentleman.'

'But I don't want to marry her,' gasped Perry.

'What?' said Reggie.

'What?' exclaimed the Duke.

'What?' added Marjorie and Ursula, almost in unison.

'*Ils sont très drôles, les anglais, n'est-ce pas?*' said the Frenchman in the crowd.

'I'm too young to get married,' explained Perry, plaintively, 'I'm only eighteen.'

'D'you mean to say you refuse to make an honest woman of my wife?' asked Reggie, trying to get the facts straight in his mind.

'Well, I'm not going to marry her, if that's what you mean,' said Perry petulantly.

'I must say I agree with the boy. Most unsuitable liaison,' put in the Duke, unwisely.

Reggie looked closely into Perry's face and then turned and stared at the Duke.

'Horse shit, both of you,' he said. Before anyone could do anything sensible, he had picked up Perry as if he were a child and tossed him into the Grand Canal, and then turned, seized the Duke, and sent him flying after his son. The sight of a real Duke and his only son and heir surfacing, spluttering, in the Grand Canal was, I must confess, such a rarity that I savoured it to the full. Two carabinieri, who until then had been standing in the crowd quietly enjoying the drama as any true Italian would, now, with the utmost reluctance, decided that, as representatives of law and order, they ought to make some sort of a gesture. Elegant as peacocks they drifted up to Reggie.

'Pardon, signor,' said one of them in excellent English, 'but are you having any trouble?'

It was Reggie's big moment and I was lost in admiration at the way that he rose to the occasion.

'It is kind of you to ask, but I do not require assistance,' he said regally, if unsteadily. 'My wife has been seduced by the son of a Duke. I am here to take my wife back home shince I now believe her to be cured of her infatuation. The Duke and his son are that strange couple you see disporting themselves in the Canal there. I have no wish to prefer charges against them. Come, Marjorie, let us away.'

So saying he took the by then bewildered and submissive Marjorie by the hand and walked off through the crowd, leaving me with a very damp and angry Duke and his son and two courteous but interested members of the Italian police force. It took us two hours to explain what it was all about, who the Duke was, who Perry was, who I was, who Ursula was and who (if they could only have been found) Reggie and Marjorie were. In addition we had to vouchsafe all the extra information that the bureaucratic machine demands: date of birth, whether our grandmothers had in-growing toenails and so on. Eventually, limp with exhaustion, we left the Duke and his sulky son and heir, and Ursula and I repaired to a pleasant bar on the Piazza San Marco.

'Darling, I do think you handled that *wonderfully*,' she said, her big blue eyes melting as she gazed at me. 'You handled those awful policemen with such aplumb.'

'Aplomb,' I corrected automatically.

'That as well,' she agreed. 'I was so proud of you.'

'Thank you,' I said, 'what'll you have to drink?'

'I'll have a Graffiti,' she said, 'with ice.'

'Madam will have a Martini and ice and I'll have a double brandy and soda,' I translated for the waiter.

'I'm so glad that I managed to sort out Reggie's problem,' said Ursula, with satisfaction.

'I was under the impression that he solved his own problem.'

'Oh, no, darling,' explained Ursula. 'If it hadn't been for me and the Duke, and, of course, all *your* help, Reggie wouldn't have known what to do.'

'Why don't you stop trying to help your friends?' I asked. 'Why don't you just leave them alone?'

'You can't just leave them *alone*,' said Ursula. 'You don't know *what* they're going to do when you leave them alone . . . Now, you must admit that if I hadn't taken part in the whole affair Reggie and Marjorie wouldn't be happily together again. In this instance I was a sort of catapult.'

'Catalyst?' I suggested.

'I do wish you would stop trying to correct me, darling,' said Ursula. 'I think you're ravishing but this constant correcting becomes very irritating.'

'You think I'm ravishing?' I asked, intrigued.

'I always thought you were ravishing, but I really don't see what that's got to do with Reggie and Marjorie,' said Ursula hurriedly.

'Frankly, at this precise moment, I am unmoved by anything that may, or may not, happen to Reggie and Marjorie in the future. I feel they deserve each other. I feel that the Duke and his son ought to get married and, to encapsulate the whole incredibly futile affair in a nutshell, I came to Venice to enjoy myself and you are a very beautiful woman. So why don't we stop talking about the incredibly dull landed gentry of England, and you tell me what we are going to do tonight . . . and I warn you, it's got to be sexy.'

Ursula went pink, partly with embarrassment and partly with pleasure.

'Well, I don't know,' she said, to my unmitigated delight. 'I had thought of going to bed early.'

'Darling, you *couldn't* have suggested anything better,' I exclaimed with enthusiasm.

'You know perfectly well what I mean,' she went on, bridling.

'Now that you have solved the various problems of Reggie, Marjorie, Perry and the Duke,' I said, 'why don't you relax? Come and have a disgustingly sexy dinner with me and then decide whether or not you want to spend the next two days of your stay in Venice in that squalid pension of yours or whether you want to have a bedroom the size of a ballroom overlooking the Grand Canal.'

'Ooool' she said. 'You haven't got a bedroom looking out over the Grand Canal . . . you perfect *pig*.'

'Why don't you go back to your hotel and change, and I will go back to my hotel and try to get them to resurrect this suit, and I will then pick you up at seven thirty. By that time, I feel, you can have made up your mind whether or not you are going to exchange your squalid abode for one of the finest bedrooms in Venice.'

We had a splendid dinner, and Ursula was at her best. While

we dawdled over coffee and brandy, I asked her whether she had given any thought to her change of abode.

'Darling, you are *romantic*,' she said archly, 'just like Pasadouble.'

'Who?' I asked, puzzled.

'You know, the great Italian lover,' she said.

'You don't mean Casanova?' I asked, out of interest.

'Darling, you're correcting me again,' pointed out Ursula, coldly.

'I'm so sorry,' I said contritely, 'but I'm terribly flattered that you should think I am as romantic as Pasadouble.'

'You always were romantic in a peculiar sort of way,' said Ursula candidly. 'Tell me, is your bedroom *really* as big as that and does it *really* look out over the Grand Canal?'

'Yes to both questions,' I said ruefully, 'but I must confess that I would be happier if your motivation was based on my personal charms rather than the size and site of my bedroom.'

'You *are* romantic,' she murmured vaguely. 'Why don't we go back to your hotel for a night cap and look at your room?'

'What a splendid idea,' I agreed heartily. 'Shall we walk?'

'Darling, now you're being unromantic,' she said. 'Let's go by water.'

'Of course,' I said.

She insisted on a gondola, rather than a speedboat.

'You know,' she said sighing luxuriously, 'I've only been in Venice for four nights but I've had a gondolier every night.'

'Don't tell a soul,' I said, kissing her.

In her sweeping white dress she looked so attractive that even the gondolier (a notoriously hard-bitten and cynical breed of mammal) was impressed.

'Darling,' said Ursula, pausing theatrically in the lamp light on the jetty, 'I think I'm going to enjoy our affair.'

So saying she went to get into the gondola, broke the heel off her shoe and fell head first into the Canal. I would, with only a modicum of gentlemanly concern have let her struggle out of the water on her own (since I knew she could swim like an otter), but the voluminous dress she was wearing – as soon as it got wet – wrapped itself round her legs and, doubling its weight with water, dragged her down. There was nothing for it: I had to shed my coat, kick off my shoes and go in after her. Eventually, having inadvertently drunk more of the canal water than I thought necessary or prudent, I managed to get her to shore where the gondolier helped me to land her.

'Darling, you were brave to rescue me . . . I do hope you didn't get too wet,' she said.

'Scarcely damp,' I said, getting her into the gondola.

By the time we got to the hotel she was shivering, and so I made her take a hot bath. By the time she had done this she was running a temperature. In spite of her protests that there was nothing wrong with her I made her go to bed in my ballroom-sized bedroom. By midnight her fever was such that I was seriously worried and called a doctor, a sleepy and irritated Italian who did not appear to have ever come within spitting distance of the Hippocratic oath. He gave her some tablets and said she would be all right. The next day I procured a doctor of my own choice and discovered that Ursula had pneumonia.

I nursed her devotedly for two weeks until the medical profession agreed that she was well enough to travel. Then I took her down to the airport to see her off. As the flight was called she turned to me, her huge blue eyes brimming with tears.

'Darling, I did so enjoy our affair,' she said. 'I hope you did too.'

'I wouldn't have missed it for the world,' I agreed, kissing her warm mouth.

Even Passadouble, I felt, could not have been more tactful than that.

THE HAVOC OF
HAVELOCK

Coming from a family which treated books as an essential ingredient of life, like air, food and water, I am always appalled at how little the average person seems to read or to have read. That the dictators of the world have always looked upon books with mistrust had appeared to me peculiar, for books, I considered, provided a myriad of friends and teachers. That books could influence people, I knew – *The Origin of Species, Das Kapital*, the Bible – but to what extent a book could wreak havoc was never really brought home to me until I introduced Havelock Ellis to the Royal Palace Highcliffe Hotel.

On arrival in Bournemouth, I had made my way as rapidly as possible to my favourite bookshop, H. G. Cummin in Christchurch Road. Here, in a tall, narrow house, is housed a vast and fascinating collection of new and second-hand books. On the ground floor and in the basement all the new books glare at you somewhat balefully in their multicoloured dust-jackets, but climb the creaking, uneven staircase to the four floors above, and you are transported into a Dickensian landscape. Here, from floor to ceiling in every room are amassed arrays of old books. They line the walls of the narrow staircases, they surround you, envelop you, a wonderful, warm, scented womb.

Pluck the books out, and each smells different. One smells not only of dust but of mushrooms; another, autumn woods or broom flowers in the hot sun, or roasting chestnuts; and some have the acrid, damp smell of coal burning; and others smell of honey. And then, as if smells alone were not enough, there is the feel of them in the heavy leather bindings, sleek as a seal, with the golden glitter of the type buried like a vein in the glossy spine.

Books the dimensions of a tree trunk, books as slender as a wand, books printed on paper as thick and as soft as a foxglove leaf, paper as white and as crisp as ice, or as delicate and brittle as the frost layer on a spider's web. Then the colours of the bindings: sunsets and sunrises, autumn woods aflame, winter hills of heather; the multicoloured, marbled end-papers like some Martian cloud formation. And all this sensuous pleasure to drug and delight you before you have even examined the titles: (*The Great Red Island – Madagascar*; *Peking to Lhasa*; *Through the Brazilian Wilderness*; *Sierra Leone – its People, Products and Secret Societies*), and come to the splendid moment when you open the book as you would a magic door.

Immediately the shop around you disappears and you stand, smelling the rich smell of the Amazon with Wallace, you bargain for ivory with Mary Kingsley, you face a charging gorilla with du Challu, you make love to a thousand beautiful women in a thousand novels, you march to the guillotine with Sidney Carton, you laugh with Edwardian gentlemen in a boat, you travel to China with Marco Polo; all this you do standing on the uneven, uncarpeted floor, with a magic passport in your hands, without the expenditure of a penny. Or perhaps I should say one *can* do this without the expenditure of a penny, but I seem incapable of entering a bookshop empty-handed or of leaving it in the same condition. Always, my cheque book is slimmer, and I generally have to order a taxi to transport my purchases.

On this particular occasion, I had already spent much more than I had intended (but who if he has any resolve in his make-up, strength in his character, can refuse to buy a book on Elephants or the Anatomy of The Gorilla?), when I suddenly saw, squatting peacefully on a shelf level with my eyes (so I could not possibly miss it) a series of volumes I had long wanted to acquire. This set was bound in a dark maroon coloured cloth and, apart from the difference in the thickness of each volume, they were identical. The title, in block, was so obscure as to be almost unreadable, and indeed I might easily have missed this Pandora's box of books if a stray shaft of winter's sunlight had not wandered through the dusty window at that precise moment and illuminated the volumes and their titles: *The Psychology of Sex*, by Havelock Ellis.

Now, anyone who studies, keeps or, most important, breeds, rare animals knows how important sex is, and the study of sexual impulses in an animal which can talk and write of its experiences and feelings – the human animal, man – is of enormous help in the study of the less articulate members of the animal kingdom. Though I possessed a fairly extensive library on the subject of human sex, it was lacking one master work for which I had been searching for some time – the classic Havelock Ellis, to a large extent now superseded by modern research but still an important early study on that subject, and certainly a wealth of information.

The young lady who helped me carry the books downstairs obviously thought that a man of my age should not be buying nine volumes on the subject of sex. John Ruston, the owner of the shop who had known me for a good many years, was more sympathetic.

'Yes,' he said, swaying to and fro like a dancing bear. 'Yes, Ellis. We don't get him in often.'

'I've been trying to find him for ages,' I replied. 'I'm delighted.'

'It's a nice, clean copy,' said John, with unconscious humour, picking up the volume dealing with homosexuality and examining it.

So my Havelock Ellis was packed up, together with a few last-minute purchases (who, with red blood in his veins, could resist *The Speech of Monkeys*, or *A Slave Trader's Journal*, or *The Patagonians?*), and John Ruston had me driven round to the hotel where, for the next week, I devoted myself almost exclusively to Havelock, carrying him around, a volume at a time, and marking with a pencil those parts which I thought applicable to animal breeding generally. What I didn't realize was that, at mid-winter in a nearly deserted hotel, my movements were studied by the staff about as carefully as I studied my own animals. What they saw was me deeply absorbed in a book (since all the volumes looked much the same), in which I kept marking passages as I drifted from cocktail bar to restaurant, from restaurant to deserted lounge. When they brought up my breakfast at seven-thirty, I was lying in bed reading Havelock and the night porters would find me still engrossed in him at two o'clock in the morning. Obviously there must be something about the book that kept me riveted and silent for such long periods.

I was totally unaware of the interest that my absorption with Havelock was arousing, until Luigi, the Italian barman, said to me:

'That seems to be a very interesting book you are reading, Mr Durrell.'

'It is,' I said vaguely. 'Havelock Ellis.'

He said no more, not wishing to confess that he did not know who Havelock Ellis was. Then Stephen Grump, the Viennese Under-Manager, said to me:

'That seems to be an interesting book you are reading.'

'Yes,' I said. 'Havelock Ellis.'

He, too, not wishing to appear ignorant, merely nodded his head wisely.

So enchanted was I, not only by the research work that

Havelock had done, but by the character that seemed to emerge from his prose – earnest, pedantic, humourless, as only Americans can be when they take a subject seriously; an omelette made up of the meticulousness of a Prussian officer, the earnestness of a Swedish artist, and the cautiousness of a Swiss banker – that I was oblivious of the fact that all around there were people who were dying to know what I was reading. The dull red cover, the almost undecipherable title, gave them no clue. Then one day, quite by accident, my secret was out, and immediately pandemonium broke loose on a scale that I had rarely seen equalled. It all happened quite innocently in the restaurant, where I was reading Havelock as I demolished an avocado pear and an excellent lasagne (for the restaurant was exclusively run by Italians though some of the kitchen staff were English). In between mouthfuls of pasta heavily laced with Parmesan cheese, I was reading Havelock on the different aspects of beauty in women, and what attracts and does not attract in different parts of the world. I came to a phrase used in Sicily which I suspected would provide much food for thought if only I had the remotest idea what it meant.

Irritatingly, Havelock assumed that everyone spoke fluent Italian and so there was no footnote with a translation. I puzzled over the phrase for a moment and then recalled that the head waiter, Innocenzo, was from Sicily. Little realizing I was setting alight the fuse that led to a powder keg, I called him over to my table.

'Is everything all right?' he enquired, his large hazel eyes flashing round the table to make sure.

'Delicious,' I said. 'But that's not what I called you for. You said you came from Sicily, didn't you?'

'Yes, from Sicily,' he nodded.

'Well, can you just translate that for me?' I asked, pointing to the relevant passage.

It had a curious and quite unprecedented effect on him. His

eyes widened unbelievingly as he read. Then he glanced at me, walked away from the table a few steps in embarrassment, came back, read the passage again, looked at me, and retreated from the table as though I had suddenly grown another head.

'What is that book?' he asked me.

'Havelock Ellis. *The Psychology of Sex.*'

'You read it now for one week,' he said accusingly, as though he'd caught me in some underhand dealing.

'Well, there *are* nine volumes,' I protested.

'Nine?' he exclaimed. '*Nine?* All on sex?'

'Yes. It's a big subject. But what I'm interested in is whether this is true. Is this what you say about women in Sicily?'

'Me? No, *no!*' said Innocenzo, hurriedly, living up to his name. 'Me, I never say that.'

'Never?' I asked, disappointed.

'Maybe sometimes my grandfather may have said it,' said Innocenzo, 'but not now. Oh, no, no! Not *now.*' He gazed at the books fascinated. 'You say this man write nine books?' he asked again. 'All on the sex?'

'Yes,' I said. 'Every aspect of it.'

'And this is what you are reading all this week?'

'Yes.'

'So now you are an expert,' he said, laughing embarrassedly.

'No, he's the expert. I'm just learning.'

'Nine books,' he repeated wonderingly, and then dragged his mind back to his job. 'You want some cheese, Mr Durrell?'

'No, thank you,' I said. 'Just some more wine.'

He brought a bottle, uncorked it, and poured out a drop for me to taste, his eyes fixed fascinatedly on the book. I approved the wine, and he poured it out.

'Nine books,' he mused, carefully untwisting the cork from the corkscrew. 'Nine books on sex. *Mama Mia!*'

'Yes,' I concluded. 'Havelock did the job properly.'

Innocenzo left me, and I returned to Havelock, earnest and meticulous in his investigations among the hot-blooded

Sicilians. Meanwhile, unbeknownst to me, my hot-blooded Sicilian had passed on to the waiters the news that Mr Durrell possessed nine volumes on sex, surely a record for any hotel guest. The news spread through the hotel like fire through summer gorse-land. When I returned from a shopping expedition that afternoon, two of the porters rushed to open the doors of the hotel for me, and behind the desk not one but four receptionists blinded me with their smiles, their faces as pretty as a flower-bed. I was somewhat startled by all this sudden enthusiasm, but, in my innocence, did not connect it with my owning Havelock Ellis. I went up to my room, ordered some tea, and lay on the bed reading. Presently, my tea was brought to me by the floor waiter, Gavin, a tall, slender boy with a delicate profile, a mop of blond hair like the unkempt mane of a Palomino, and large blue eyes.

'Afternoon,' he said, his eyes fixed on my book.

'Good afternoon, Gavin,' I said. 'Just bung it on the table, will you?'

He put the tea on the table and then stood looking at me.

'Yes?' I asked. 'Do you want something?'

'Is that your dirty book, then?'

'Dirty book!' I replied, indignantly. 'This is Havelock Ellis; the definitive work on the psychology of sex. Dirty book, indeed!'

'Well, that's wot I mean,' said Gavin. 'Sex.'

'Sex – contrary to what the English think – is not dirty,' I pointed out, with some asperity.

'Naw, well . . . you know . . . I know it's not,' said Gavin. 'But, well . . . Imeantersay . . . everyone else thinks so, don't they?'

'Fortunately, there is a small minority that holds other views,' I retorted. 'You among them, I trust.'

'Oh, yeah. Imeantersay, I'm all in favour of it, like. What I say is, let everyone do what they like, more or less,' said Gavin, adding, 'providing it's not somefing you're not supposed to do

. . . you know, like drugging girls and sending them off to Buenos Aires and places like that . . . that sort of thing.'

'Yes, even in sex one should have fair play,' I agreed gravely.

He twisted the napkin he carried in his hands and sighed gustily. It was obvious that he had a problem.

'Wot's it say, then?' he asked at last.

'About what?'

'About sex, of course.'

'Which particular aspect?'

'Wot you mean? Aspect?' he asked, puzzled.

'Well, do you want to know about ordinary sex, or lesbianism, homosexuality, sadism, masochism, onanism?'

' 'Ere!' interrupted Gavin. 'Does 'e write about all those? Honest?'

'Yes,' I said. 'It's all sex in one shape or form.'

'Gawd Almighty!' exclaimed Gavin, with feeling. 'Yeah . . . well, I suppose you're right. Live and let live is wot I say.'

'Quite.'

Gavin tied a knot in the napkin and beat it against the palm of his hand. It was obvious he was dying to ask something.

'Have you a problem?' I asked.

Gavin jumped.

'Who me?' he cried, backing away towards the door. 'No, no! I've got no problem. Not me. Not a problem.'

'So, Dr Havelock Ellis can't help you?' I enquired.

'Oh, no,' said Gavin. 'Imeantersay . . . I got no problems. Not like wot some people 'ave . . . I'll be back for your tray presently. All right?'

He made a hasty exit.

By now, I judged, the whole hotel would be throbbing, as a jungle throbs with talking drums, with the news of Havelock Ellis. I sipped my tea and waited expectantly. Within the hour, Gavin was back.

'Enjoy your tea?' he asked.

He'd never asked this before.

'Yes, thank you,' I said, and waited.

There was a pause while he juggled the tea tray dexterously on to one palm.

'Read any more, then?' he asked at last.

'A few pages.'

He blew out his cheeks and sighed.

'I suppose it's a good book to read if you've got . . . well, problems?'

'Very soothing,' I said. 'He treats everything sensibly, and doesn't give you a guilt complex.'

'Yeah, well . . . that's good. It's bad to have a complex, isn't it?'

'Detrimental. Very detrimental.'

Silence fell. He shifted the tray from his right hand to his left.

'Yeaa . . .' he said, thoughtfully. 'I got a friend wot's got a complex.'

'Really? What sort of complex?'

'Well, it's sort of difficult to explain, like; he's quite a good-looking fella, like . . . Well, Imeantersay, 'e's not bad-looking, ya know. I mean, all the girls like 'im. In fact, to tell ya the truth, there's, er, two of 'em wot's come ta blows over 'im,' he said, with modest satisfaction. 'Two of them Portuguese chambermaids . . . Yea, didn't arf hurt each other. Pulled each other's hair and punching each other. 'Ot tempered, these foreigners are, don't ya think?'

'Very,' I said. 'Is that your friend's problem? Too many hot-blooded Portuguese girls to take to bed?'

'No, no! No . . . no . . . it's not that. 'E don't like 'em, see.'

'You mean, he's got a girl-friend already?'

'No, no! Wot I'm saying . . . 'e don't *like* girls, see?' he blurted out, desperately. 'I mean ta say, 'e doesn't like . . . well, you know . . . muckin' about with 'em.'

'You mean he likes boys?' I asked.

He reddened.

'Well, no . . . I mean . . . well, 'e says 'e's . . . you know, mucked about with a few boys and . . . well, 'e says . . .'

His voice trailed away uncertainly.

'He says he prefers them to girls?' I enquired.

'Well . . . yeah . . . sort of. That's wot 'e *says*.'

'Well, there's nothing wrong with that. Does it worry him?'

'You mean, it's all right being . . . sorta queer, like?' he asked.

'If you're born like that, it's no sin. You can't help it, any more than you can help the colour of your eyes.'

'Oh,' he said, struck by this thought. 'No . . . I suppose ya can't really.'

'Would your friend like to borrow Havelock Ellis and see what he says about homosexuality?'

'I expect he would,' said Gavin, but slightly defensively. 'I should think he probably would. I'll . . . um, ask 'im, like, and let you know.'

'You wouldn't like to take it now, just in case?'

'Well,' he said, his eyes fastened on the book I held out. 'Well, I might just take it an' . . . if 'e doesn't want to read it . . . well, I'll . . . I'll just bring it back. All right?'

'All right,' I said. 'Tell him not to spill beer all over it.'

'Oh, no,' he said, as he made for the door with the book under his arm. 'I won't do that.'

The door closed behind my first patient.

On the fifth morning, Gavin brought my breakfast up to me. He entered the room jauntily.

'Well?' I asked. 'Did your friend derive any comfort from the book?'

'My friend?' asked Gavin, blankly.

'Yes. Your friend with the complex.'

'Oh, 'im . . . Yes, well . . . 'e said it was very interesting. I took a glance at it meself. Very interesting. Imeantersay, 'e writes about it . . . well, sensible. I mean, 'e doesn't sorta say your a bloody poof, or anything.'

'As it should be,' I agreed, sipping my tea.

'Yeah,' said Gavin. 'I'll tell you wot, though – all of them receptionists aren't arf worked up about that bit wot 'e says in there abaht lesbians.'

'You lent it to them?' I asked. 'You realize that if the manager catches you, I shall be thrown out and you'll lose your job for peddling pornographic literature.'

'Naw, 'e won't catch me,' said Gavin, with fine scorn.

'Well, what did the receptionists say?' I enquired, wondering if it would ever be safe for me to venture downstairs again.

'Ya know Sandra? The blonde one? The one wot's quite good looking? Well, she shares a flat with Mary . . . Mary, the one wot's rather fat, with glasses. Well, after reading wot 'e says in that book, Sandra says she's goin' to get 'er own flat. She says she wondered why Mary always wanted to scrub 'er back in the bath, and now she knows, and she's not 'aving none of that. Mary's ever so cut up about it . . . crying all over the place and saying she's not a lesbian. She says it's very difficult for people to keep their own backs clean, and she's only trying to be 'elpful; but Sandra says she's got enough trouble with 'er boy-friends without 'aving Mary in the bath with 'er.'

'She's got a point there,' I said, judiciously. 'And what about the other two?'

'Aw, well, ol' Miss 'Emps, she says she'd share a flat with Mary, cos she liked having 'er back scrubbed and didn't see any 'arm in it. And Sandra said Miss 'Emps was tryin' to seduce Mary, and so Miss 'Emps got ever so angry an' said she'd rather have 'er back scrubbed by a girl than 'er front scrubbed by a man, which is wot Sandra seemed to like. So Sandra got livid and said she was just as much a virgin as Miss 'Emps, but she stayed that way 'cos she wanted to, while Miss 'Emps was virgin 'cos she *'ad* to be. So none of 'em is speaking to each other now.'

'I'm not surprised,' I observed. 'Don't you think you ought to take them the volume on pure motherhood?'

'Naw, they'll be all right,' said Gavin. 'Does 'em good, a bit of a row; clears the air.'

'But it also deprives Mary of her one pleasurable activity,' I pointed out.

'She'll be all right,' said Gavin. 'They're all going to a party tonight, so that'll be OK for 'em.'

'Are you going to this party?' I asked, hoping for a first-hand report.

'Naw,' said Gavin, looking me in the eye with a certain pugnacity. 'I'm goin' out with me friend, Rupert.'

'Well, have a good time.'

'You bet I will,' said Gavin, as he swaggered from the room.

Later that day, when I went to cash a cheque at the reception desk, they were all red-eyed and tight-lipped. I was treated with a frigid courtesy that would have intimidated a polar bear. However, Havelock had not yet completed the full cycle of havoc. Soon I had a steady flow of patients. There was the young porter, Dennis, a nice but regrettably unattractive Scots lad, made more so by two physical defects. He had a speech impediment and a fine and fiery relief-map of acne across his face, from which his round brown eyes peered shyly. He brought me a telegram and then stood fidgeting in the doorway.

'N-n-n-no reply, sir?' he asked.

'No thank you, Dennis.'

'Is there anything else I c-c-can g-**g**-get you, sir?'

'Not at the moment. Not unless you have an exceptionally pretty sister of loose morals.'

'N-n-n-no, sir. My sister's m-m-married, sir.'

'Good for her,' I said, heartily. 'It's nice to know that the old institution's still surviving. It's as heart-warming as finding a dinosaur.'

'That b-b-b-book you lent Gavin, sir . . . Does it say much about m-m-marriage, sir?'

'Havelock says a lot about marriage,' I said. 'What had you in mind?'

'Does he say anything about p-p-p-prop-p-posing, sir?'

'Proposing marriage? Well, I'm not sure. I don't think he gives any definite instructions. It's more a general account of how to behave after you're married.'

'But you h-h-have to p-p-p-propose first, sir,' he pointed out.

'Of course. But that's easy enough. Who do you have in mind to propose to?'

'S-s-s-s-s-andra,' he said, and my heart sank. Sandra was the last girl for him, even if he looked a million dollars which, with his acne and his chin covered with yellow down like a newly-hatched pigeon, he certainly did not. Add to this his impediment, and his chances of winning Sandra's hand were about equal to his chances of becoming Prime Minister.

'Well, it's simple enough,' I said heartily. 'You take her out, give her a good time, and then, at the end of the evening, you pop the question. Simple. It's after she says "yes" that your difficulties begin.'

'I've got s-s-s-spots,' said Dennis, dolefully.

'Everyone's got spots,' I replied. 'I'm not going to disrobe for you, but I've got spots all over my whole back. It looks like an aerial photograph of the higher peaks of the Andes.'

'That's on your b-b-b-back,' pointed out Dennis. 'M-m-mine are on my f-f-face.'

'It's scarcely noticeable,' I lied. 'I wouldn't have seen them if you hadn't drawn my attention to them.'

'I s-s-stammer,' he said. 'How can you p-p-p-propose if you s-s-stammer?'

'A slight impediment,' I reassured him firmly. 'When you come to the great moment, you'll be so excited you'll forget to stammer.'

'I b-b-blush, too,' went on Dennis, determined to lay out all his faults for my examination.

'Everyone blushes,' I pointed out. 'Even I blush, but you can't see it because of my beard and moustache. It shows a nice, delicate nature. It's nothing to be ashamed of. Actually Havelock has a bit about blushing in volume eight.'

'Does he s-s-say anything about s-s-s-stammering and s-s-spots?' asked Dennis, hopefully.

'Not spots. That's really not his scene. Do you want to borrow this to read what he says?'

'Yes, p-p-please,' said Dennis, eagerly.

He seized volume eight and scuttled off with it. The whole interview had left me feeling as limp as a psychiatrist at the end of a heavy day. I hoped that Havelock would produce a panacea for Dennis, for he was a nice, earnest boy, but I doubted it; the dice were too heavily loaded against him.

The next person to seek the advice of Havelock was Giovanni, one of the restaurant waiters, a tall, handsome, sleek, dark man, like a well-groomed antelope with melting eyes. He looked so supremely full of self-confidence that it was hard to believe he had any problems at all, let alone sexual ones. But he waited one lunch time until I had lingered rather long over my meal and was the last person in the restaurant, then took up a station within six feet of my table and stared fixedly at me until I stopped writing.

'Yes?' I sighed. 'What's your problem, Giovanni?'

'Well,' he said, coming forward eagerly. 'I justa wanta aska you . . . thata book, er . . . she tells you about sadism?'

'Yes,' I said. 'Why? Do you feel an overwhelming urge to beat up Innocenzo?'

'No, no! It's notta me. It is-a my girl-friend.'

'Oh,' I said cautiously. 'What's the problem?'

He glanced around furtively to make sure we were alone.

'She bitas,' he said, in a hushed whisper.

'She bites?'

'Yessa.'

'She bites what?' I asked, slightly confused, as this was the last thing I had expected.

'She bita me,' he explained.

'Oh!' I felt somewhat at a loss, for even Havelock had not prepared me for a girl who bit large Italian waiters.

'What does she bite you for?'

'She say I tasta good,' he said, solemnly.

'Well, isn't that a good thing?'

'No. Itta hurts,' he pointed out. 'Soma-tima I'm afraid she bita veina, and I bleeds to death.'

'Surely not. You couldn't bleed to death from a few love-bites.'

'It is notta few love-bitas,' he said, indignantly. 'She issa sadism.'

'A sadist,' I corrected.

'She's thatta too,' he agreed.

'But love-bites are very common,' I explained. 'They are really a sign of affection, of love.'

He glanced round once more to make sure we were alone, then unbuttoned his shirt.

'Issa thissa love, or is she sadism?' he enquired, displaying to me a chest covered with an astrakhan-like pelt of fur, through which could be seen several neat red circles of teeth marks. In several places the skin had been broken, and at one point a piece of sticking-plaster was applied.

'Well, it may be painful,' I commented, 'but I don't really think it qualifies as sadism.'

'No?' he queried, indignantly. 'Whatta you wanta that she should do? Eata me?'

'Why don't you bite her back?' I suggested.

'I cannot do. She would not like it.'

He certainly seemed to have a problem and his chief problem was that he had no idea what a real sadist was.

'Would you like to borrow the book that talks about sadism?' I asked. 'Would that help?'

'Yessa,' he beamed. 'Then I reada it to her, and she will see she is a sadism.'

'Well, I wouldn't read it all to her,' I said, in a precautionary way. 'After all, you don't want to start her on whips and things.'

'I reada it first,' he said, after a moment's thought.

'Yes, I would just censor it first if I were you. I'll bring it down this evening, Giovanni.'

'Thanka you, Mr Durrell,' he said, and bowed me out while re-buttoning his shirt.

Two days later, he returned the book, looking worried.

'Is all aright,' he whispered.

'Good,' I said. 'What happened?'

'She thoughta when I'm reading her these things he say, thata I wanta to do it to her. So she say, "no, no way". So I say "you willa give up being sadism, and I willa too".'

'And she agreed?'

'Yessa. She agree.'

'And does it work?'

'Lasta night,' he said, closing one eye and looking at me. 'Lasta night, she was gentle like a bird, like a beautiful bird . . . so softa.'

'Very nice,' I said.

'No. She is angry with me.'

'Why?' I asked, puzzled.

'She was so beautiful, so softa, so gentle, that I bit-a her,' he confessed. 'Now she say she no sleepa with me again.'

'She'll change her mind,' I reassured him, comfortingly. But he looked doubtful, and by the time I left the hotel his beautiful biter had not given in to his importuning.

In the unfortunate case of the kitchen porter and the cellar-man, I was, quite unwittingly (with the aid of Havelock), the cause of some upset, of which, I am glad to say, the only really detrimental aspect was that the soup of the day, minestrone, was burnt black. It started because I'd found a short-cut through the cellars underneath the hotel, which led me straight out on to the cliffs instead of having to walk along miles of road.

Here, since my short-cut led past the dustbins, I would frequently meet the kitchen porter or the cellarman. The porter was a nice Irish lad, with a lazy smile, very blue eyes, a crop of auburn hair and a face freckled as thickly as a blackbird's egg. In direct contrast, the cellarman was a rather dark, saturnine individual, whose face, in repose, looked sulky but was transfigured when he smiled. He had a most attractive, deep, husky voice with a real Dorset accent. The news of my apparent endless fund of sexual knowledge (as represented by Havelock Ellis), filtered down into the cellars and both these attractive young men brought their troubles to me. The first one was the cellarman, David.

'You see, sur,' he confessed, blushing slightly. 'I think she's bloody wonderful. 'Ur knows I do; 'ur knows I want to marry 'ur. But 'ur won' let me do it, sur. Not no which way. But 'ur durn't want me to do it with anyone else, see? Not tha' I want to, understand? But what I say is, either she do it wi' me, or I does it wi' some'un else. Fair's fair, sur, don' you think?'

'She thinks abstinence makes the heart grow fonder,' I said, and regretted it when he gave me a reproachful look.

'It's no jokin' matter, sur. It's gettin' me down, 'onest. I wunnered if thur was anythin' in your book, like, I could give 'ur to read? Sort of, well . . . encourage 'ur, I suppose.'

'I'll lend you the volume on sexual education and abstinence,' I promised. 'Though I don't guarantee the results.'

'Of course not, sur. I unnerstand,' he said. 'I jus' want somethin' to git 'ur started, like.'

So I lent him volume six.

Next, I was approached by the auburn-haired Michael. He had exactly the same problem with his girl-friend. I reflected that we were supposed to live in a promiscuous and permissive society, and yet everyone in the hotel seemed to behave like early Victorians. Certainly the girls appeared to cling to their maidenheads with the tenacity of limpets.

'I'm afraid you'll have to wait in the queue, Michael,' I said.

'I have just lent the volume you want to David.'

'Oh, him. Sure, he's a bloody wash-out,' said Michael. 'I didn't even know he had a girl. He doesn't even look as though he'd the strength for a pee, let alone anything else.'

'Well, he has a girl, and he's suffering just as you are. So, show some sympathy.'

'It's sympathy I'm needing,' he replied. 'This girl's driving me mad. She's ruining me health. Even me religion is suffering and that's a terrible thing to do to an Irishman.'

'How is she affecting your religion?' I asked, astonished by this revelation.

'Sure, an' I've nothing to confess,' he said, indignantly. 'And Father O'Malley won't believe me. The other day, he asked me what I had to confess, and when I said "nothing, Father", he told me to say fifty Hail Marys for lying. The shame of it!'

'I'll give you the book the moment I get it back,' I promised. 'With luck, it might help you *and* David.'

How was I to know that they were courting the same girl, since neither of them knew it either?

I had been for a walk along the cliffs, visiting that monstrously macabre monument to bad taste, the Royal Coates Museum and Art Gallery, and was taking my short-cut back into the hotel when I came upon an arresting tableau. Michael and David faced each other, each puce in the face, Michael with a bleeding nose and David with a cut on his forehead, being held back from attacking each other again by the rotund chef and his second-in-command. Face downwards on the ground lay my precious copy of Havelock, and nearby lay the trampled, blood-stained chef's hat and the wickedly sharp meat cleaver. I rescued my book as the two antagonists still strained to get at each other and yelled abuse. I gathered, from the incoherent mouthings of both of them, that Michael had been shown Havelock by his girl-friend and, knowing it could only have come from one source, had laid in wait for David and chased him with the meat cleaver. David, being agile, had dodged the cleaver, hit Michael on the nose, and run for it. Michael had flung a bottle at him and hit him on the forehead. Before they could get to grips, however, they had been pulled apart by the two chefs.

'Don't you think you are behaving stupidly?' I enquired.

'Stupidly?' roared Michael. 'With that creeping Protestant toad giving filthy books to my Angela!'

'*Your* Angela!' snarled David. ' 'Ur's not your Angela; 'ur's as good as said she'll marry *me*. An' it's not a filthy book, neither. It's Mr Durrell's.'

'She wouldn't marry you, you Protestant carrion. And if that's not a filthy book, may I never breathe again,' said Michael. 'If you'll excuse me sayin' so, Mr Durrell, you ought to feel a wave of shame, so you ought, at having helped this conniving bastard to try and despoil one of the fairest and daintiest girls I've ever seen outside Ireland. May God strike me dead if it's not the truth.'

'But you wanted to borrow the book to give to Angela yourself,' I pointed out.

'Sure! An' it's all right for me; I'm her fiancé,' said Michael.

I knew better than to argue with Irish logic.

'Listen,' I said. 'I don't mind you fighting and killing each other; that's your affair. You're both equally guilty, since you both wanted the book for the purpose of getting Angela to bed. You ought to be ashamed of yourselves. I will not have my property flung about like this. If I report this to the manager, then you'd both get the sack and neither of you would be able to marry Angela. Anyway, I don't think either of you stand a chance. I saw her out at dinner last night with Nigel Merryweather.'

Nigel was a handsome young director of the hotel.

'Nigel Merryweather?' said Michael. 'That swine! What's she doin' with him?'

'Merryweather?' said David. 'She said 'ur didn't like 'im.'

'Yes,' agreed Michael. 'She said he made her feel sick.'

'Well, there you are,' I concluded. 'It looks as though you've both had it.'

'That settles it,' said Michael. 'I've finished with women. Like a bleedin' monk I'll be livin' from now on.'

'After all I did for 'ur,' complained David. 'To play me false with Merryweather, who makes 'ur feel sick, like she told me.'

A strong smell of burning now started to emanate from the kitchen.

'Holy Mary, Mother of God!' said Michael.

'My minestrone! My minestrone! You bloody bog Irish,' screamed the chef, and he grabbed Michael's arm and hauled him back into the kitchen at a run.

The second chef, Charlie, a rubicund cockney from Hammersmith, relinquished his hold on the other heart-broken lover.

'I don't know what to think about 'ur, I really don't,' said David.

'Don't think,' I advised. 'Go and have a drink and tell Luigi to put it on my bill.'

'You're very kind, sur,' he said, brightening, as he moved towards the upper floors and the bar.

'Lucky you came along when you did,' said Charlie, when David had disappeared. 'They were all set to kill each other, silly idiots – using a bleedin' meat cleaver, an' all.'

'Tell me,' I asked, 'who is Angela?'

Charlie stared at me for a moment. 'You mean to say . . .?' he began. Then he started to laugh.

'Well, I had to say *something*,' I explained, 'or we'd have been here all day.'

'An' I suppose you never seen no Nigel Merryweather neither?' he chortled.

'I haven't *seen* him,' I said, 'but I was told he was the most handsome of the younger directors, with something of an eye for the girls, and no shortage of cash.'

'Quite right,' said Charlie. 'A regular gun dog, 'e is.'

'Gun dog?' I asked, puzzled.

'Ah, yes, you know, always after the birds.'

'Yes,' I agreed. 'Gun dog. What a good description. Well, all's well that ends well.'

'Tell me,' said Charlie. 'Wot was that book they was all so excited about?'

I explained. 'It's an excellent series of volumes when used properly,' I said, 'but in this place, everyone who reads them seems to go berserk.'

'Would it give advice on marriage in wot one would call an . . . intimate way?' asked Charlie, a pensive look in his eye.

My heart sank. 'Well . . . yes,' I said, 'but you must remember that it's sort of a text-book really.'

'Yes,' went on Charlie. 'It might be just wot I want. A text-book – like a school-book, you might say?'

'Oh, dear. Are you sure?'

'Well,' said Charlie confidentially. 'Me an' the missus 'aven't been rubbin' along too sharp recently. She's been a bit depressed, like – an' a bit naggy, if you get my meaning. Nothin's right. She went to see one of those blue phonographic films a couple o' weeks back, an' now she says I don't do it right. She says it's the same old way every time and it's drivin' 'er mad. She says I 'aven't got no imagination. I told 'er she wasn't no Kama-bleedin'-Sutra, neither – but she says it's all my fault.'

'Well, it could be.'

'Now, this book of yours . . . does it tell you about them things? You know, different ways, and such like?'

'Yes,' I said, cautiously.

'Well, then – can I borrow it for a bit?' he pleaded. 'To improve me technique, like?'

How could I resist this pudgy, middle-aged man pleading for the text-book to improve his passionate overtures to his wife? It would have been sheer cruelty.

'All right,' I said, resignedly. 'I'll lend you volume two.'

'Thank you, sir.' He grinned. 'Cor! I'll bet this'll liven the old girl up. I'll bet she'll be ever so pleased.'

He was wrong. Two days later, as I was having lunch, he limped out of the kitchen and came over to my table, carrying volume two. His right eye was half-closed and swollen and of an interesting series of colours ranging from purple on his cheek-bone to scarlet and pink around his eyebrow.

'Hello,' I said. 'What have you done to your eye?'

He laid Havelock on the table with care.

'I never done it,' he said. 'It's the old woman wot's done it. After all that nag, nag about bleedin' sex, she up and catches me a wollop like a bleedin' pile-driver. And d'you know why, sir?'

'Why?' I asked, fascinated.

He sighed, the weary sigh of a man faced by a woman's logic. ' 'Cos I brought a dirty book into the house, sir. That's why,' he said.

I decided that Havelock had caused quite enough problems and so I would call in all the volumes I had out on loan. Besides, I was leaving in twenty-four hours and, such was the success of Havelock as light reading, I was afraid that I might not get all the books back.

I had just been round the hotel leaving messages for Dennis, Gavin and Stella (a chambermaid who was worried about her boy-friend: 'All 'e ever thinks about is sex. Honest, 'e doesn't even take an interest in football.'), when I ran into the manager, Mr Weatherstone-Thompson.

'Ah! Good afternoon, Mr Durrell,' he said. 'I understand that you are leaving us the day after tomorrow?'

'Yes, alas,' I said, 'I have to get back to Jersey.'

'Of course, of course, you must be so busy with all your gorillas and things,' he laughed unctuously. 'But we *have* enjoyed having you here.'

'And I've enjoyed being here,' I replied, backing towards the lift.

'And the staff will all miss you,' said Mr Weatherstone-Thompson, adroitly getting between me and the lift, 'and I think they will even miss your little . . . Ha, ha! . . . library.'

I groaned inwardly, Mr Weatherstone-Thompson was an overweight, wheezing, always-slightly-moist fifty, who smelt strongly of whisky, Parma violets and cheap cigars. He was married to a suicide blonde (dyed by her own hand) some twenty-five years his junior. She did not just have an eye for the men, she had a seine net out for them. Mr Weatherstone-Thompson had problems, but I was not going to let him borrow Havelock to solve them. Skilfully, I got round him and in line with the lift again.

'Oh, yes, Havelock Ellis,' I said. 'A most interesting series of volumes.'

'I'm sure, I'm sure,' said Mr Weatherstone-Thompson eagerly. 'I was wondering if perhaps, when the rest of the staff have finished . . . er . . . drinking at this fountain of knowledge, if I might . . .'

'Oh, what a pity!' I said, remorsefully. 'You should have told me before. I've just packed them up and sent them on ahead to Jersey.'

His disappointment was pathetic, but I hardened my heart. 'Oh,' he said. 'Oh, well. Never mind. It can't be helped. What I always say is that that sort of book is interesting in its way, but really, if you're an experienced man like you and I are . . . well, there's not much it can teach us.'

'No, indeed,' I said, 'I should think it would take more than a book to add to *your* knowledge.'

Mr Weatherstone-Thompson laughed and his eyes brightened as he mentally reviewed his imaginary prowess.

'Well, I'll not deny I've had my moments,' he said, chuckling.

'I'm sure you have,' I agreed, as I got into the lift. 'In fact, you should be writing the books, not reading them.'

I left him (Casanova, Mark Antony, Ramon Navarro rolled into one) laughing protestingly at my compliment to his powers as a seducer.

By the following morning I had retrieved all my Havelock

Ellis except the one I had lent to Gavin. Havelock, I found, was still weaving his spell. Dennis confessed that he was now thoroughly confused. Before Havelock, he had always thought there was only one sort of sex and that was chaste and pure. Stella said that, instead of Havelock making her boy-friend take an interest in football, it made him worse than ever, and she had had a terrible time the previous night retaining her virginity.

It only remained to get back the volume I had lent Gavin. This was the one dealing with normal sex, since Gavin had been working his way steadily through all nine volumes. They told me that he had gone up to Sheffield for the week-end but was due back the Monday morning I was supposed to leave.

The morning of my departure dawned bright and clear and I was awakened by the door of the passage-way leading into the suite opening, followed by a thump. Then the door closed again. I thought perhaps they had brought my breakfast.

'Come in,' I called sleepily, but there was no response. I decided it was probably some over-enthusiastic chambermaid, waiting to do out the room at the crack of dawn, rolled over and went back to sleep again.

It was not until I got up later to go and have a bath that I saw the copy of Havelock Ellis lying just inside the doorway in the hall. So it had been Gavin I had heard, returning volume eight. As I picked it up, a note fell out.

'Thanks for book,' it said. 'Wish I'd never borrowed the bloody thing. Lent it to Rupert and got back to find him in my bed with a girl. Am giving up sex. Yours truly, Gavin.'

Havelock, game to the last, had struck his final blow.

THE MICHELIN MAN

———————◆———————

Many years ago, when I first started to travel in France, a kindly friend pressed a copy of the Guide Michelin into my hands, rather in the spirit that prompts the Gideon Society to fill lonely hotel bedrooms with copies of the Bible. The Guide Michelin (known affectionately as 'the Mich') is to a traveller and gourmet what the Bible is to a Christian, the Koran to a Mohammedan or the sayings of Buddha to a large section of the world. It is your guide, mentor and friend when travelling in France. It is small, fat and red – like so many cheerful French peasants you see who have become well-padded and polished over the years by good food and wine. Within its scarlet covers are the dossiers of some two thousand hotels, pensions and restaurants, their innermost secrets revealed.

A glance at the Mich and you know every reasonable hostelry within a fifty-mile radius of your position. It tells you whether the hostelry in question allows dogs in your room, whether they are *'tout confort'* or dismissed as merely being acceptable; whether they have garages, telephones, private baths and other adjuncts of modern living; whether they are quiet (a red rocking chair as the inspired symbol) or whether they have a *'jardin fleuri'*.

But in addition to this almost Scotland Yard dossier on each place the Mich does something more: it tells you about food.

France is an eminently sensible country where people take food seriously as an art form, which indeed the cooking and presentation of food is; an art form which has, unfortunately, become almost extinct in Britain. In France the choice of a dish is made with the same care as you would employ in choosing a wife, and in some cases even greater. Therefore the Mich has printed in its margins against the various restaurants certain symbols that guide and succour the person who takes food and its preparation seriously.

The first symbol is a small etching of crossed spoon and fork. One of these denotes a plain but adequate meal, two or three mean comfortable or very comfortable while four crossed spoons and forks mean the presentation is of exquisite excellence. After this the mind becomes bedazzled.

Four crossed spoons and forks accompanied by a star mean you will have an ambrosial meal in ideal circumstances and are on the first rungs of the gastronomic ladder that leads to that Paradise where you discover a place with four crossed spoons and forks and *three* stars. There are, however, only four of these in France. Getting three stars in the Mich is considerably more difficult than obtaining the Victoria Cross, the Croix de Guerre or the Purple Heart, and to get even *one* is an achievement that would make any serious chef die happy.

Once you have assessed the culinary worth of a place by the spoons, forks and stars in the margin you may then move on to something else which the Michelin company thoughtfully provides. Under each entry they list the specialities of the restaurant and the wines of which they are particularly proud. This means that – having chosen your place of refuge – you can then spend five minutes or so getting your taste buds overexcited by reading the list of specialities that are provided for your delectation, toying mentally with gratin of fresh-water crayfish tails, or turbot poached in cream, lobster soup, or a Charolais steak accompanied by *cèpes*, those marvellous wild mushrooms, black as sin, that look as though they should be witches' umbrellas.

The Guide, therefore, is not merely a guide book, it is a gastronomic experience. Only once did I doubt this incomparable volume. Only once did I think – for a brief moment – that, in its zeal to leave no gastronomic stone unturned, the Mich might have overstepped the canons of good behaviour. This was some years ago when I was paying my annual pilgrimage to a small house I have in the South of France, to which I repair to try to pretend that Alexander Bell has never invented the telephone and to get some writing done.

That year Europe had crept out from under a warm, wet winter into a riotous, multicoloured fragrant spring. France, always one of the most beautiful of countries was, in consequence, like a magnificent piece of embroidery, ashine and aglitter with flowers so that the countryside was as ravishing and as multicoloured as a Fabergé Easter egg. It was the time of the mustard as I headed south and so the car drifted down country lanes that meandered through a landscape as yellow as a nest of canaries, a delicate but bold yellow. So enraptured was I at the flower-bedecked hedges and banks, the vast yellow fields of mustard, the tiled roofs of the cottages looking in the vivid spring sunshine as crisp as gingerbread, that I drove in a sort of daze.

At noon I stopped in a village that encompassed some fifty souls and bought for myself wine, a fresh loaf of brown bread, a fine, brave cheese and some fruit. Then I drove on until I found a gigantic field of mustard curving over the rolling hills like a yellow carpet. Here I parked the car in the shade of some chestnut trees, took my provender and made my way into the delicate sea of yellow and green. I lay down among the fragile mustard plants and ate and drank, lapped in this sea of gold. Then, making up my mind that I must drive on, I fell deeply and peacefully asleep.

I awoke when the sun was getting low, slanting on to my bed of mustard, turning the pale yellow to old gold, and I realized

I had driven without direction, slept far too long and now had not the faintest idea where I was. It was reaching that hour of the afternoon when all intelligent travellers on the French roads pull in to the side and start consulting their Michelins. But it was useless my doing this for I did not know where I was.

I got into the car and drove slowly along the road until, by good chance, I came upon a wagon piled high with fragrant cow manure being driven by a little man who looked like an animated walnut. With great good humour he reined in his two mammoth horses and showed me on the map exactly where I was, pointing out the very spot with a calloused forefinger brown with earth and sun. I thanked him and he clopped and jingled and creaked on his way, while I got out my Mich and started looking up every town and village in a thirty-mile radius. It was a fruitless task. Each one I looked up was treated frostily by the Mich and there was nothing of any gastronomic quality at all. I had apparently struck one of those curious blank spots in France where there was nothing – so to speak – Michelinable.

Then I spotted a village on the map some twenty kilometres away, but so tiny and remote I felt sure it would have nothing. I looked it up anyway since I was attracted by its name, Bois de Rossignol, the Nightingale Wood. To my astonishment the Mich informed me (almost quivering with delight) that the village boasted one tavern, 'Le Petit Chanson' (which in view of the Nightingales struck me as being pleasantly apposite). Wonder of wonders, it not only had six rooms but baths, telephones, a garage, a red rocking chair for serenity and a *'jardin fleuri'*. In addition it had *three crossed spoons and forks and a star*. It closed for the winter but had reopened on this very day.

I read the description again, hardly believing my eyes, but there it was in black and white. Underneath the description of the amenities was the list of specialities. This riveted my attention for they would have done credit to a large hotel on the Côte d'Azur. The proprietor obviously made up his own names for his specialities, which argued a fine, free spirit. There were tails of fresh-water crayfish 'in clouds of eggs'. There was beef in red wine, 'For the Hunger of Theodore Pullini'. There was a 'Tart of Wild Strawberries for the Delectation of Sophie Clemanceau'. I was enchanted and immediately made up my mind that I must, at all costs, stay at 'Le Petit Chanson'. Slamming the Mich shut I started the car and drove with all speed to Bois de Rossignol, hoping to get there before all the other salivating gourmets on the roads should arrive before me and occupy all six rooms in the hotel.

The village, when I found it, was delightful. It consisted of some two dozen or so houses grouped amicably round a small, sunlit square, lined with huge plane trees that guarded a small and very beautiful fountain. One end of the square was dominated by a tiny and perfect little fifteenth-century church which raised an admonishing, slender spire to the gingerbread roofed houses around it. Every available space on window ledges on pavements and on the tops of walls was covered by regiments of flower pots, window boxes, tin cans and, in some cases wheel-barrows and old prams, all aglow and overflowing with spring flowers. I pulled up by a bench on which sat five old men, wizened, toothless, wrinkled as lizards, soaking up the evening sun, and asked them the way to 'Le Petit Chanson'. Eagerly a chorus of quavering voices and a forest of gnarled hazel sticks pointed me through the village and out the other side. A few hundred yards along the road I came to a side-turning at which was a sign informing me that 'Le Petit Chanson' lay to my left. The road was narrow and ran beside a baby river, green and silver in the sun, bounded on one side by woodland, and on the other by vineyards, the vines like black, many-branched arthritic candelabras each with a wig of new green leaves on top.

'Le Petit Chanson', when I came to it, was no disappointment. The road curved between two huge oak trees and there, in a garden like a patchwork quilt of flowers lay the hotel, a long low building with a red-tiled roof blotched here and there with emerald cushions of moss. The walls and part of the roof were almost invisible under one of the most flamboyant and magnificent wisterias I had ever seen. Over the years it had lovingly embraced the building, throwing coil after coil of itself round the walls and roof until the occupants had been hard pressed to keep it from barring the doors and windows. At ground level the trunk had a girth that any self-respecting python would have been proud of, and the whole complicated web of trunk and branch that had the house in its grip was as blue as a kingfisher's wing with a riot of flowers.

In a small gravel square among the flower beds in front of the hotel neat white tables and chairs were laid out in the shade of six or seven Judas trees in full bloom. Their pinky-red blooms were starting to fall; the ground was red with them and the white table tops were bespattered as by gouts of dragon's blood. Beyond the garden stretched woodland and great skyward sloping fields of mustard.

I parked the car and, carrying my overnight bag, walked into the hotel. The small hall smelt of food and wine and floor polish, and everything was clean and shining. I was first greeted by an enormous hairy dog that, had you met him in the woods, you would have been pardoned for thinking a bear. He was, however, most amiable. I soon found that he had several delicious, ticklish spots behind his ears and had him groaning with pleasure as I massaged them. Presently a young waiter made his appearance and I asked him if they had a room for the night.

'*Certainement, monsieur*,' he said with grave politeness and taking my case from me he led me down a passageway to a charming bedroom whose window was rimmed with blue wisteria framing the distant fields of mustard.

After I had bathed and changed I made my way downstairs and out into the garden, floodlit now with the rays of the setting sun. I sat down at a table and started to think hopefully that a

Pernod might be a not entirely unacceptable idea when the young waiter appeared.

'Excuse me, *monsieur*,' he said, 'but *monsieur le Patron* asks whether you will drink a bottle of wine with him, for you are the first customer we have had this year and it is his custom to celebrate like this.'

I was enchanted by such a civilized idea.

'Of course I will be delighted to accept,' I said, 'but I do hope that the *Patron* will come out and join me?'

'*Oui, monsieur*,' said the waiter, 'I will tell him.'

I was anxious to meet the *Patron* for I felt sure that he was the one responsible for the quaint names of his various specialities, and I wanted to find out why they had been thus christened. Presently he appeared. His appearance was in keeping with the name of the hotel and the whole ambience of the place. He was a giant man, some six foot three in height, with shoulders as wide and solid as a café table. His massive face with an eagle nose and brilliant black eyes, framed in a shock of white hair, belonged to an Old Testament prophet. He wore an apron which was spotless and a chef's hat perched jauntily on the back of his head and in his huge hands, the joints cobbled by arthritis, he carried a tray on which was a bottle of wine and two very beautifully-shaped glasses. He was, I judged, in his middle eighties, but gave the impression of being indestructible. You felt he would live to be well over a hundred. He beamed at me as he approached as though I was a dear friend of long standing; his eyes flashed with humour; his delighted smile was wide and his face fretted with a thousand lines that the laughter of his life had etched there.

'*Monsieur*,' he boomed as he set the tray carefully on the table, 'welcome to my hotel. You are our first guest of the season and so are especially welcome.'

He wrung my hand with courteous enthusiasm and then sat down opposite me. The force of his personality was like a blast furnace. He exuded kindness and good will and humour in equal quantities and so was irresistible.

'I do hope that you will like this wine,' he continued, pouring it out carefully into the glasses. 'It is a Beaujolais from my own little vineyard. I have enough grapes to make some twenty bottles a year, for my own consumption, you understand, and so I only open it on special occasions such as this.'

'I am honoured,' I said, raising my glass. The wine slid into my mouth like velvet and the fragrance illuminated my taste buds.

The old man rolled it round his mouth and swallowed thoughtfully. 'It is a truthful wine,' he said.

'Very truthful,' I agreed.

'You are *en vacances* here?' he enquired.

'Yes,' I said. 'I have a little house down in Provence and I try to go there every summer.'

'Ah! Provence! . . . the country of herbs,' he said, 'what a lovely area of France!'

'The whole of France is beautiful. I think it is one of the loveliest countries in the world.'

He beamed at me and nodded. We drank for a while in respectful silence that one gives to a special wine, and then the old man refilled our glasses.

'And now you wish for the menu?' he asked.

'Yes, please,' I said. 'I was reading about some of your specialities in the Michelin. You must be an excellent chef to have obtained your star.'

He closed his eyes and an expression of anguish passed for a moment across his fine face.

'Ah, the star, the star,' he groaned. 'You have no idea, *monsieur*, what I had to suffer to get that star. Wait, I will get you the menu and after you have chosen I will tell you about the star. It is, I assure you, a romance such as Dumas might have invented and yet it is all true. A moment while I get the menu.'

He went off into the hotel and returned presently with the

menu and the wine list and placed them in front of me.

'If I may venture to make a suggestion,' he said as he re-charged our glasses, 'the "Pigeons for the Sake of Marie Theresa" is something I am really proud of and I have some fine, plump, fresh squabs. As you are our first customer of the season I will, naturally, broach another bottle of my Beaujolais to accompany the pigeons.'

'You are very kind,' I said. 'The pigeons sound admirable. Tell me, I notice that you give curious names to all your specialities. I presume they have some special significance?'

'Why yes, *monsieur*,' he said gravely. 'When one invents a new dish I think it is only befitting that its name should com-memorate some event. For example, take the pigeons. I in-vented this dish when my wife was pregnant with our first child. You know the strange humours women get at such times, eh – ? Well, my wife developed a passion for tarragon and pigeons. *Enfin!* It was incumbent upon me to invent a dish that would not only feed her and our unborn child, but would appeal to the finicky appetite of a pregnant woman of great beauty and sensibility. So, I invented this pigeon dish for the sake of Marie Theresa, which is my wife's name.'

'What a fascinating idea,' I said. 'I must start doing that myself, for I am something of a cook and I always think that so many lovely dishes have the dullest names.'

'It is true. I see no reason why imagination should not go into the creation of a dish and also into the naming of it.'

I perused the menu for a few moments.

'I think,' I said at last, 'that with your "Pigeons for the Sake of Marie Theresa" as a main dish, I would like to start with the "Pâté Commemorating the passing of Albert Henri Périgord" and then finish with some cheese and perhaps "Tart of Wild Strawberries for the Delectation of Sophie Clemanceau".'

'An admirable choice, *monsieur*,' he said, getting to his feet. 'Now, please help yourself to more wine. I will just tell my wife of your wishes and then I will return and tell you the story of how we got our star.'

He went off into the hotel and presently reappeared with a dish of olives and some small but delicious cheese puffs.

'Yes, *monsieur*,' he said thoughtfully, easing himself into the chair and taking a sip of wine, slouching easily in the attitude of the professional raconteur. 'The fact that we have a star is, to my mind, a small miracle as I am sure you will agree when I tell you the full story. This all happened, of course, before the fourteen-eighteen war, for as you will have discerned, although I am a fine upstanding man, I am no longer in the first flush of youth.

'In those days I was something of an artist, albeit an un-successful one. I still dabble a bit and do the odd oil or water-colour, but I found my true artistic *métier* was in the kitchen. However, in those days, as I say, I tried to earn a few francs by doing the odd portrait and pictures of people's homes. In this way I earned a rather uneven living, but I enjoyed myself tramping through France and if no one bought my pictures I did whatever job was offered. I have mended roads, picked grapes and cherries and even been, for a short time, a snail farmer.

'Well, one spring in just such a season as this, my wanderings led me to this village. As you may imagine the countryside was looking magnificent and I was captivated by the colours and the scenery. I decided that if I could stay in this vicinity for a while I would be able to paint some really remarkable pictures. But, as was often the case with me, I had no money, so I had to set about looking for a job. As you may well believe in a village of this size jobs were as rare as a goose with five livers.'

He sighed and sipped his wine musingly. 'Well,' he continued eventually, 'there was a man in the village who had taken a fancy to me and he spoke to the proprietor of this hotel, saying what a fine fellow I was and asking him if he would consider giving me a job in the kitchens as a skivvy. The owner's name was Jean Jacques Morceau, a strange, earnest man, short and fat and much given to hysteria over small events so that you sometimes thought him more like an old maid than a man. Nevertheless, *monsieur*, Morceau cooked like an angel. I do assure you that some of his inventions tasted as though they had been transported straight down from Paradise by kind permission of *le bon Dieu*.

'His pastry was as light as cobwebs; his sauces burnt their way delicately into the very fabric of your mouth so that you thought you had been eating all the most fragrant flowers of the world. His omelette of crayfish tails and finely chopped fennel and walnuts was such a wonderful creation that I have seen men with tears of emotion running down their cheeks as they ate one. He had a white wine sauce in which he would simmer oysters and asparagus tips so that the result was so ambrosial that, if you were a person of fine sensibility and a delicate constitution, you could well faint with pleasure at the first mouthful. He had a way of stuffing wild duck with rice, pine nuts and white truffles soaked in brandy that created a flavour in your mouth as though a whole orchestra was playing: your palate rang with the music of the food. In short, *monsieur*, Jean Jacques Morceau was a gastronomic genius, a Leonardo da Vinci of the table, a Rembrandt of the taste buds, a veritable Shakespeare of the cuisine.'

The old man paused, took a sip of wine, popped an olive into his mouth and delicately spat the pip into an adjacent flower-bed.

'He also had a daughter, the most beautiful woman I have ever seen in my life, *monsieur*, and really this was the cause of all the trouble, for, having laid eyes on her, I had eyes for no other women. She was incomparable. I, who had taken my pleasures with women in a light-hearted way (and I will not conceal from you that I liked the opposite sex and indeed had considerable success with them); I, who had sworn that I would never marry; I, the gay here-today-gone-tomorrow lover; I fell so deeply in love that I behaved like a calf that has lost its mother, running about like a headless chicken, carrying on like a dog betrayed by aniseed. There was nothing, not even murder, that I would not have done to marry that girl.'

He gave a great, heartfelt sigh, raised his eyes to heaven at his ancient folly, and took another drink. 'I worked here for a year and with each of the 365 days I grew more deeply in love. What was even more extraordinary, the girl grew to love me. However, she was an only child, you understand, and so stood to inherit this hotel. Her father viewed all suitors with grave suspicion, since he felt they might well want to marry the hotel rather than the girl, in spite of her undoubted beauty. Therefore it was not surprising that we both knew that any attempt on my part to ask for her hand in marriage would be immediately misconstrued.

'We discussed it at great length, the girl and I, and we knew that to be successful we should have to move with great caution. It was then that I had my brilliant idea; at least, I thought it was brilliant at the time, but it turned out to be much more complicated than I had imagined.'

He lit a cigarette as yellow as mustard and poured out some more wine. 'At that time, *monsieur*, the Michelin tyre company had just started issuing its now world-famous Guide and awarding stars for distinguished tables. As you know the Michelin man comes in secret to your hotel or restaurant and samples your cuisine. Only when this has been done are you aware that you have been tested, so, you understand, it is necessary for you to keep up the same standard at all times, for you are never sure when a Michelin man is lurking among your customers.

'Now Jean Jacques Morceau knew that he cooked like an angel but he also felt that his hotel was a little bit too distant from the great highways to attract the attention of a Michelin man. To know that he *should* be awarded a star and yet to be convinced that he would never obtain one, drove the poor man nearly crazy. He could talk of nothing else. It became a grand obsession that ruled his whole life. At the mere mention of the Michelin Guide he would fly into an hysterical rage and start throwing things. It is true, *monsieur*, with my own eyes I saw him throw a Bombe Surprise and a Turkey en Cocotte at the kitchen wall. It was terrible for him to have an all-consuming passion like that, *but* it served my purpose admirably. You see I told him that I had heard from my uncle (in the strictest confidence, of course) that he had just been appointed as a Michelin man.'

'And *had* your uncle been appointed?' I asked.

The old man laid a forefinger alongside his nose and closed one eye.

'Of course not,' he said, 'in fact I had no uncle.'

'Then what was the point?' I asked, puzzled.

'Wait, *monsieur*, and I will unfold my whole plan to you. Naturally, when I told Morceau this he got wild with excitement, as I knew he would, and did his best to persuade me to get my uncle to come and stay. At first I said that it would be unethical and I could not possibly expect my uncle to do anything like that. This went on for a week or so, with Morceau doing his best to get me to change my mind. Then, when I had driven him to a near frenzy, I weakened. I said that, even if I did get my uncle down, I could not promise that he would award the hotel a star. Morceau said he quite understood this but that all he wanted was the chance to show his prowess in the kitchen. I expressed doubt about the whole project and kept him on tenterhooks for another few days. Then I said that I was in love with his daughter and she with me and if I agreed to get my uncle down he would have to agree to our getting betrothed. As you may imagine, this threw him into an hysterical fury. A newly made Tarte aux Pommes missed me by a hair's breadth, and I did not dare venture into the kitchen for the rest of that day. However, as I had hoped, his obsession with the star was too strong and the following day and with the utmost reluctance he agreed to us getting engaged. The day after I put the engagement ring on her finger I went up to Paris to see my uncle.'

'But you said you hadn't an uncle,' I protested.

'No, *monsieur*, I had no real uncle, but I had a substitute one, an old friend of mine called Albert Henri Périgord. He was the black sheep of a well-to-do family and he lived in a garret on the left bank of the Seine, painting a little, swindling a little and generally living on his wits. He had special qualities which I needed: he was of a very aristocratic and haughty mien, he knew a lot about food and wine which he had learnt from his father who was something of a gourmet, and lastly, he was enormously fat – in a way that you would expect a Michelin man to be – and could eat and drink more than any other human being I had met in my life. He engulfed food, *monsieur*, as a whale engulfs little shrimps, or so I am told.

'I went to Paris, called at the garret of Albert Henri and found him, as usual, without a sou to his name and (since he always was) ravenously hungry. I took him out to dinner and unfolded my plan to him. I said that I wanted him to come down here for a week, posing as my uncle, and then to take his leave and return to Paris. There he would write a polite note to Morceau saying that he would do what he could about a star but could promise nothing, as the final decision was not his: he could merely recommend.

'Needless to say Albert Henri was enchanted by the idea of a trip to the country and a week of eating as much as he could want, prepared by a culinary genius such as Morceau. I sent a telegram to Morceau telling him my uncle was coming down for a week and then Albert Henri and I went down to the Flea Market and got him some respectable second-hand clothes, for he had to look like a man of substance. Mind you, it was not easy, *monsieur*, for Albert Henri must have weighed every gramme of a hundred kilos. But at length we managed to fit him out with something and this, combined with his aristocratic bearing, made him look every millimetre the Michelin man he was supposed to be.

'We finally arrived down here to find my future father-in-law in a state of hysterical delight. He treated Albert Henri as if he were Royalty. I had warned Morceau, of course, that he was at no time to mention to my uncle that he knew he was a Michelin man, and I had warned Albert Henri not to divulge this information to Morceau.

'To see them together, *monsieur*, was a delight: the more Morceau fawned on Albert Henri the more haughty and regal did Albert Henri become, and the more regal he became the more Morceau fawned on him. My future father-in-law had gone to unprecedented lengths to ensure success. The kitchen had been scrubbed until every copper pot and pan shone like a harvest moon. The larder was stuffed to capacity with every sort of fruit and vegetable, every form of meat and game. More, in case he might suddenly find that he did not have the necessary ingredients to satisfy the "Michelin man's" every whim, my future father-in-law had taken the unprecedented and expensive step of having a car and a chauffeur at the ready so that they could dash, post-haste, into the nearest big town to procure whatever it was that this exalted guest might demand.'

The old man paused and chuckled reminiscently as he sipped his wine. 'Never have I seen such cooking, *monsieur*, and never have I seen such eating. Morceau's genius was in full flower, and the dishes that flowed from the kitchen were more complicated, more beautifully balanced, more delicious in aroma, texture, than anything that he had ever produced before. Of course, this made Albert Henri's genius for over-eating come to fruition. They vied with each other, *monsieur*, like two armies fighting for supremacy. As the dishes became more and more ambrosial Albert Henri would order more and more dishes for each meal, until he was having six and seven courses, not counting the sweet and cheese, of course.

'If the eating was a Herculean task, washed down by rivers of wine, the preparing of the food was also a mammoth undertaking. Never have I worked so hard, in spite of the fact that we had engaged three temporary skivvies to do the vegetables and so forth. Morceau was like a man demented: he flung himself around the kitchen like a Dervish, screaming instructions, chopping, stirring, tasting and occasionally running, panting, into the dining-room to watch Albert Henri stuffing food into himself in such prodigious quantities that one could hardly believe one's eyes. A word of praise from Albert Henri and Morceau would go purple with pleasure and gallop back to the kitchen to fling himself with renewed enthusiasm into the task of creating another dish more splendid than the last.

'I assure you, *monsieur*, that when he cooked his version of Lièvre Royale – and it took two days in the making – the aroma was such that they could smell it down in the village and all the villagers, to a man, trooped out here just to stand in the garden so that they could have the privilege of simply *smelling* the dish. It was when all this activity was at its height, when Albert Henri's appetite appeared to get more gargantuan with each meal that he (just having consumed some comfit of goose of incredible richness and fragrance) rose to his feet to toast the blushing Morceau . . . and dropped dead.'

The old man sat back and watched my expression with satisfaction.

'Great heavens!' I exclaimed. 'What did you do?'

The *Patron* looked grave and stroked his chin.

'I will not conceal from you the gravity of the situation, *monsieur*,' he said. 'Look at all the ramifications. If a doctor was called in it would lead to the eventual discovery that Albert Henri was *not* a Michelin man, and this might lead to Morceau putting an end to my engagement with his daughter, for in those days children obeyed their parents, especially the girls. This I could not allow. Fortunately at the moment when Albert Henri crashed to the floor there was only my future father-in-law and myself in the room. I had to think fast. Needless to say, Morceau had gone into a sort of hysterical decline when he discovered that Albert Henri was dead and so were his chances of getting a star. To get him in the right mood I pointed out the full horror of the situation: he had, with his culinary art, *actually killed a Michelin man.* If he had any hopes of ever getting a mention in the Michelin Guide, let alone getting a star, this dreadful fact must be kept from the Michelin company at all costs.

'Even in the condition he was in, weeping hysterically, he saw the wisdom of my words. What, he implored me, were we to do? *Mon Dieu*, I could not tell him that I had about as much idea of what to do as he had. I had to take the initiative or else the whole situation would disintegrate.

'Firstly, I said, he must dry his eyes, gain some control over himself and then go into the kitchen and send his daughter to her room, saying that she had been over-working (which was perfectly true). He must dismiss the kitchen boys, say that Monsieur Albert Henri Périgord had a headache and was retiring to bed. On no account was anyone to be allowed into the dining-room.

'Having tidied him up a bit – for in his frenzy of grief he had torn off his chef's hat and trampled it underfoot and hurled a bottle of excellent Medoc at the wall, a lot of which had splashed over him – I sent him into the kitchen. Then I dragged the body of Albert Henri out of the dining-room through the hallway and down into the cellar which, being cool, we used for keeping our wines and game and poultry. I went back upstairs to find that Morceau had done everything that I had suggested, so that we had a moment's respite.

'Morceau was beginning to show signs of considerable strain and I knew that he would break under it if I did not keep him occupied. I opened a bottle of champagne and made him drink. In his highly excited state the wine had a befuddling effect which calmed him down considerably. We sat there like two criminals, *monsieur*, discussing the best way of getting rid of a corpse weighing over a hundred kilos. It was a macabre discussion I can assure you.

'Morceau was all for waiting until it was dark and then taking the body out in the pony and trap and leaving it in some remote forest glade a number of kilometres from the village. I objected to this on the score that, if the body *was* discovered, people in the village knew of Albert Henri's presence in the hotel and would ask why his body should be found so far away. This would immediately throw suspicion on Morceau. Did he, I asked, want to be known throughout the length and breadth of France as the chef who had killed a Michelin man with his cooking? He burst into tears again and said he would commit suicide if this was said of him.

'I said that we must be intelligent and think of a way of disposing of the corpse without implicating ourselves. I told him that my "uncle" was unmarried and had only a small circle of acquaintances, so that his disappearance would not occasion any undue alarm. This was indeed true, for Albert Henri *had* a very small circle of acquaintances simply because he was so untrustworthy. I knew that anyone in Paris would treat his disappearance as a cause for rejoicing rather than the reverse. I could hardly tell Morceau that, so to keep him calm, I assured him that, given the hours of darkness, I would think of a solution to our problem. But I do assure you, *monsieur*, I was at my wits' end what to do.'

At this moment the waiter approached the table and told me that my food was ready.

'Good, good,' said the old man, 'don't delay. Come, *monsieur*, let me conduct you to the dining-room.'

He rose and led me into the hotel and thence into a small but beautifully appointed dining-room and there pulled a chair for me to sit down. The waiter came forward bearing a dish of toast and a large dish of pâté. A sudden realization came to me.

'Tell me,' I said to the *Patron*, 'this pâté commemorating the Passing of Albert Henri Perigord . . . is this named after your friend?'

134

'Of course, *monsieur*,' said the Patron. 'It was the *least* I could do.'

I cut a slice of the pâté from the dish, applied it to a fragment of toast and put it in my mouth. It was delicious beyond belief.

'Magnificent, *Patron*,' I said, 'a wonderful pâté. Your friend would have been proud to have had it called after him.'

'Thank you, *monsieur*,' he said bowing.

'But, tell me,' I went on, 'you haven't finished your story. You can't leave me in mid-air like that . . . what did you do with the body?'

The old man looked at me and hesitated for a moment, as if making up his mind whether to vouchsafe this secret or not. At last he sighed.

'*Monsieur*,' he said, 'we did the only thing we could do . . . indeed the only thing that I am sure Albert Henri would have wanted us to do.'

'What was that?' I asked, perhaps obtusely.

'We turned my friend into a pâté, *monsieur*. It is perhaps somewhat ironical that it was for this very pâté that we were awarded our star by the Michelin, but we were most grateful for it, nevertheless. *Bon appetit, monsieur*.' Chuckling, he turned and made his way out to the kitchen.

THE ENTRANCE

My friends Paul and Marjorie Glenham are both failed artists or, perhaps, to put it more charitably, they are both unsuccessful. But they enjoy their failure more than most successful artists enjoy their success. This is what makes them such good company and is one of the reasons that I always go and stay with them when I am in France. Their rambling farmhouse in Provence was always in a state of chaos, with sacks of potatoes, piles of dried herbs, plates of garlic and forests of dried maize jostling with piles of half-finished water-colours and oil-paintings of the most hideous sort, perpetrated by Marjorie, and strange, Neanderthal sculpture which was Paul's handiwork. Throughout this market-like mess prowled cats of every shade and marking and a river of dogs from an Irish wolfhound the size of a pony to an old English bulldog which made noises like Stephenson's *Rocket*. Around the walls in ornate cages were housed Marjorie's collection of Roller canaries, who sang with undiminished vigour regardless of the hour, thus making speech difficult. It was a warm, friendly, cacophonous atmosphere and I loved it.

When I arrived in the early evening I had had a long drive and was tired, a condition that Paul set about remedying with a hot brandy and lemon of Herculean proportions. I was glad to have got there for, during the last half hour, a summer storm had moved ponderously over the landscape like a great black cloak and thunder reverberated among the crags, like a million rocks cascading down a wooden staircase. I had only just reached the safety of the warm, noisy kitchen, redolent with the mouth-watering smells of Marjorie's cooking, when the rain started in torrents. The noise of it on the tile roof combined with the massive thunderclaps that made even the solid stone farmhouse shudder, aroused the competitive spirit in the canaries and they all burst into song simultaneously. It was the noisiest storm I had ever encountered.

'Another noggin, dear boy?' enquired Paul, hopefully.

'No, no!' shouted Marjorie above the bubbling songs of the birds and the roar of the rain, 'the food's ready and it will spoil if you keep it waiting. Have some wine. Come and sit down, Gerry dear.'

'Wine, wine, that's the thing. I've got something special for you, dear boy,' said Paul and he went off into the cellar to re-appear a moment later with his arms full of bottles, which he placed reverently on the table near me. 'A special Gigondas I have discovered,' he said. 'Brontosaurus blood I do assure you, my dear fellow, pure prehistoric monster juice. It will go well with the truffles and the guinea-fowl Marjorie's run up.'

He uncorked a bottle and splashed the deep red wine into a generously large goblet. He was right. The wine slid into your mouth like red velvet and then, when it reached the back of your tongue, exploded like a firework display into your brain cells.

'Good, eh?' said Paul, watching my expression. 'I found it in a small *cave* near Carpentras. It was a blistering hot day and the *cave* was so nice and cool that I sat and drank two bottles of it before I realized what I was doing. It's a seducing wine, all right. Of course when I got out in the sun again the damn stuff hit me like a sledgehammer. Marjorie had to drive.'

'I was so ashamed,' said Marjorie, placing in front of me a black truffle the size of a peach encased in a fragile, feather-light overcoat of crisp brown pastry. 'He paid for the wine and then bowed to the *Patron* and fell flat on his face. The *Patron* and his sons had to lift him into the car. It was disgusting.'

'Nonsense,' said Paul, 'the *Patron* was enchanted. It gave his wine the accolade it needed.'

'That's what you think,' said Marjorie. 'Now start, Gerry, before it gets cold.'

I cut into the globe of golden pastry in front of me and released the scent of the truffle, like the delicious aroma of a damp autumn wood, a million leafy, earthy smells rolled up into one. With the Gigondas as an accompaniment this promised to be a meal for the Gods. We fell silent as we attacked our truffles and listened to the rain on the roof, the roar of thunder and the almost apoplectic singing of the canaries. The bulldog, who had, for no apparent reason, fallen suddenly and deeply in love with me, sat by my chair watching me fixedly with his protuberant brown eyes, panting gently and wheezing.

'Magnificent, Marjorie,' I said as the last fragment of pastry dissolved like a snowflake on my tongue. 'I don't know why you and Paul don't set up a restaurant: with your cooking and Paul's choice of wines you'd be one of the three-star Michelin jobs in next to no time.'

'Thank you, dear,' said Marjorie, sipping her wine, 'but I prefer to cook for a small audience of gourmets rather than a large audience of gourmands.'

'She's right, there's no gainsaying it,' agreed Paul, splashing wine into our glasses with gay abandon. A sudden prolonged roar of thunder directly overhead precluded speech for a long minute and was so fierce and sustained that even the canaries fell silent, intimidated by the sound. When it had finished Marjorie waved her fork at her spouse.

'You mustn't forget to give Gerry your thingummy,' she said.

'Thingummy?' asked Paul, blankly. 'What thingummy?'

'You *know*,' said Marjorie, impatiently, 'your thingummy . . .

138

your manuscript . . . it's just the right sort of night for him to read it.'

'Oh, the manuscript . . . *yes*,' said Paul, enthusiastically. 'The *very* night for him to read it.'

'I refuse,' I protested. 'Your paintings and sculptures are bad enough. I'm damned if I'll read your literary efforts as well.'

'Heathen,' said Marjorie, good-naturedly. 'Anyway, it's not Paul's, it's someone else's.'

'I don't think he *deserves* to read it after those disparaging remarks about my art,' said Paul. 'It's too good for him.'

'What is it?' I asked.

'It's a very curious manuscript I picked up . . .' Paul began, when Marjorie interrupted.

'Don't tell him about it, let him read it,' she said. 'I might say it gave *me* nightmares.'

While Marjorie was serving helpings of guinea-fowl wrapped in an almost tangible aroma of herbs and garlic, Paul went over to the corner of the kitchen where a tottering mound of books, like some ruined castle, lay between two sacks of potatoes and a large barrel of wine. He rummaged around for a bit and then emerged triumphantly with a fat red notebook, very much the worse for wear, and came and put it on the table.

'There!' he said with satisfaction. 'The moment I'd read it I thought of you. I got it among a load of books I bought from the library of old Doctor Lepître, who used to be prison doctor down in Marseilles. I don't know whether it's a hoax or what.'

I opened the book and on the inside of the cover found a bookplate in black, three cypress trees and a sundial under which was written, in Gothic script *'Ex Libras Lepître'*. I flipped over the pages and saw that the manuscript was in long-hand, some of the most beautiful and elegant copperplate handwriting I had ever seen, the ink now faded to a rusty brown.

'I wish I had waited until daylight to read it,' said Marjorie with a shudder.

'What is it? A ghost story?' I asked curiously.

'No,' said Paul uncertainly, 'at least, not exactly. Old Lepître is dead, unfortunately, so I couldn't find out about it. It's a very curious story. But the moment I read it I thought of you, knowing your interest in the occult and things that go bump in the night. Read it and tell me what you think. You can have the manuscript if you want it. It might amuse you, anyway.'

'I would hardly call it amusing,' said Marjorie, 'anything but amusing. I think it's horrid.'

Some hours later, full of good food and wine, I took the giant golden oil lamp, carefully trimmed, and in its gentle daffodil-yellow light I made my way upstairs to the guest room and a feather bed the size of a barn door. The bulldog had followed me upstairs and sat wheezing, watching me undress and climb into bed. He now lay by the bed looking at me soulfully. The storm continued unabated and the rumble of thunder was almost continuous, while the dazzling flashes of lightning lit up the whole room at intervals. I adjusted the wick of the lamp, moved it closer to me, picked up the red notebook and settled myself back against the pillows to read. The manuscript began without preamble.

March 16th 1901. Marseilles.

I have all night lying ahead of me and, as I know I cannot sleep – in spite of my resolve – I thought I would try to write down in detail the thing that has just happened to me. I am afraid that setting it down like this will not make it any the more believable, but it will pass the time until dawn comes and with it my release.

Firstly I must explain a little about myself and my relationship with Gideon de Teildras Villeray so that the reader (if there ever is one) will understand how I came to be in the depths of France in mid-winter. I am an antiquarian bookseller and can say, in all modesty, that I am at the top of my profession. Or perhaps it would be more accurate to say that I *was* at the top of my profession. I was even once described by one of my fellow booksellers – I hope more in a spirit of levity than of jealousy – as a 'literary truffle hound', a description which I suppose, in its amusing way, does describe me.

A hundred or more libraries have passed through my hands, and I have been responsible for a number of important finds; the original Gottenstein manuscript, for example; the rare 'Conrad' illustrated Bible, said by some to be as beautiful as the *Book of Kells*; the five new poems by Blake that I unearthed at an unpromising country house sale in the Midlands; and many lesser but none-the-less satisfying discoveries, such as the signed first edition of *Alice in Wonderland* that I found in a trunk full of rag books and toys in the nursery of a vicarage in Shropshire and a presentation copy of *Sonnets from the Portuguese*, signed and with a six-line verse written on the fly-leaf by both Robert and Elizabeth Browning.

To be able to unearth such things in unlikely places is rather like water divining, either you are born with the gift or not; it is not something you can acquire, though most certainly, with practice, you are able to sharpen your perceptions and make your eye keener. In my spare time I also catalogue some of the smaller and more important libraries, as I get enormous pleasure out of simply *being* with books. To me the quietness of a library, the smell and the feel of the books, is like the taste and texture of food to a gourmet. It may sound fanciful, but I can stand in a library and hear the myriad voices around me as though I was standing in the middle of a vast choir, a choir of knowledge and beauty.

Naturally, because of my work, it was at Sotheby's that I first met Gideon. I had unearthed in a house in Sussex a small but quite interesting collection of first editions and, being curious to know what they would fetch, had attended the sale myself. As the bidding was in progress I got the uncomfortable feeling that I was being watched. I glanced around but could see no one whose attention was not upon the auctioneer. Yet, as the sale proceeded I got more and more uncomfortable. Perhaps this is too strong a word, but I became convinced that I was the object of an intense scrutiny.

At last the crowd in the saleroom moved slightly and I saw who it was. He was a man of medium height with a handsome but somewhat plump face, piercing and very large dark eyes and smoky-black, curly hair, worn rather long. He was dressed in a well-cut dark overcoat with an astrakhan collar, and in his elegantly gloved hands he carried the sales catalogue and a wide-brimmed dark velour hat. His glittering, gypsy-like eyes were fixed on me intently, but when he saw me looking at him the fierceness of his gaze faded, and he gave me a faint smile and a tiny nod of his head, as if to acknowledge that he had been caught out staring at me in such a vulgar fashion. He turned then, shouldered his way through the people that surrounded him and was soon lost to my sight.

I don't know why but the intense scrutiny of this stranger disconcerted me, to such an extent that I did not follow the rest of the sale with any degree of attention, except to note that the items I had put up fetched more than I had anticipated. The bidding over, I made my way through the crush and out into the street.

It was a dank, raw day in February, with that unpleasant smoky smell in the air that augurs fog and makes the back of your throat raw. As it looked unpleasantly as though it might drizzle I hailed a cab. I have one of those tall, narrow houses in Smith Street, just off the King's Road. It was bequeathed to me by my mother and does me very well. It is not in a fashionable part of Town, but the house is quite big enough for a bachelor like myself and his books, for I have, over the years, collected a small but extremely fine library on the various subjects that interest me: Indian art, particularly miniatures; some of the early Natural Histories; a small but rather rare collection of books on the occult; a number of volumes on plants and great gardens, and a good collection of first editions of contemporary novelists. My home is simply furnished but comfortable; although I am not rich, I have sufficient for my needs and I keep a good table and very reasonable wine cellar.

As I paid off the cab and mounted the steps to my front door I saw that, as I had predicted, the fog was starting to descend upon the city. Already it was difficult to see the end of the street. It was obviously going to turn out to be a real pea-souper and I was glad to be home. My housekeeper, Mrs Manning, had a bright and cheerful fire burning in my small drawing-room and, next to my favourite chair, she had, as usual, laid out my slippers (for who can relax without slippers?) and on a small table all the accoutrements for a warming punch. I took off my coat and hat, slipped off my shoes and put on my slippers.

Presently Mrs Manning appeared from the kitchen below and asked me, in view of the weather, if I would mind if she went home since it seemed as if the fog was getting thicker. She had left me some soup, a steak and kidney pie and an apple tart, all of which only needed heating. I said that this would do splendidly, since on many occasions I had looked after myself in this way.

'There was a gentleman come to see you a bit earlier,' said Mrs Manning.

'A gentleman? What was his name?' I asked, astonished that anyone should call on such an evening.

'He wouldn't give no name, sir,' she replied, 'but said he'd call again.'

I thought that, in all probability, it had something to do with a library I was cataloguing, and thought no more about it. Presently Mrs Manning reappeared, dressed for the street. I let her out of the front door and bolted it securely behind her, before returning to my drink and the warm fire. My cat Neptune appeared from my study upstairs, where his comfortable basket was, gave a faint mieouw of greeting and jumped gracefully on to my lap where, after paddling with his forepaws for a short while, he settled down to dream and doze, purring like a great tortoiseshell hive of bees. Lulled by the fire, the punch and the loud purrs of Neptune, I dropped off to sleep.

I must have slept heavily for I awoke with a start and was unable to recall what it was that had awakened me. On my lap Neptune rose, stretched and yawned as if he knew he was going to be disturbed. I listened but the house was silent. I had just decided that it must have been the rustling scrunch of coals shifting in the grate when there came an imperious knocking at the front door. I made my way there, repairing, as I went, the damage that sleep had perpetrated on my neat appearance, straightening my collar and tie and smoothing down my hair which is unruly at the best of times.

I lit the light in the hall, unbolted the front door and threw it open. Shreds of mist swirled in, and there standing on the top step was the curious, gypsy-like man that I had seen watching me so intently at Sotheby's. Now he was dressed in a well-cut evening suit and was wearing an opera cloak lined with red silk. On his head was a top hat whose shining appearance was blurred by the tiny drops of moisture deposited on it by the fog which moved, like an unhealthy yellow backdrop, behind him. In one gloved hand he held a slender ebony cane with a beautifully worked gold top and he swung this gently between his fingers like a pendulum. When he saw that it was I who had opened the door and not a butler or some skivvy, he straightened up and removed his hat.

'Good evening,' he said, giving me a most charming smile that showed fine, white, even teeth. His voice had a peculiar husky, lilting, musical quality that was most attractive, an effect enhanced by his slight but noticeable French intonation.

'Good evening,' I said, puzzled as to what this stranger could possibly want of me.

'Am I addressing Mr Letting . . . Mr Peter Letting?'

'Yes. I am Peter Letting.'

He smiled again, removed his glove and held out a well manicured hand on which a large blood opal gleamed in a gold ring.

'I am more delighted than I can say at this opportunity of meeting you, sir,' he said, as he shook my hand, 'and I must first of all apologize for disturbing you at such a time, on such a night.'

He drew his cloak around him slightly and glanced at the damp, yellow fog that swirled behind him. Noting this I felt it incumbent upon me to ask him to step inside and state his business, for I felt it would hardly be good manners to keep him standing on the step in such unpleasant weather. He entered the hall, and when I had turned from closing and bolting the front door, I found that he had divested himself of his hat, stick and cloak, and was standing there, rubbing his hands together looking at me expectantly.

'Come into the drawing-room, Mr . . .' I paused on a note of interrogation.

A curious, childlike look of chagrin passed across his face, and he looked at me contritely.

'My dear sir,' he said, 'my dear Mr Letting. How excessively remiss of me. You will be thinking me totally lacking in social graces, forcing my way into your home on such a night and then not even bothering to introduce myself. I do apologize. I am Gideon de Teildras Villeray.'

'I am pleased to meet you,' I said politely, though in truth I must confess that, in spite of his obvious charm, I was slightly uneasy, for I could not see what a Frenchman of his undoubted aristocratic lineage would want of an antiquarian bookseller such as myself. 'Perhaps,' I continued, 'you would care to come in and partake of a little refreshment . . . some wine perhaps, or maybe since the night is so chilly, a little brandy?'

'You are very kind and very forgiving,' he said with a slight bow, still smiling his beguiling smile. 'A glass of wine would be most welcome, I do assure you.'

I showed him into my drawing-room and he walked to the fire and held his hands out to the blaze, clenching and unclenching his white fingers so that the opal in his ring fluttered like a spot of blood against his white skin. I selected an excellent bottle of Margaux and transported it carefully up to the drawing-room with two of my best crystal glasses. My visitor had left the fire and was standing by my bookshelves, a volume in his hands. He glanced up as I entered and held up the book.

'What a superb copy of Eliphas Levi,' he said enthusiastically, 'and what a lovely collection of *grimoires* you have got. I did not know you were interested in the occult.'

'Not really,' I said, uncorking the wine. 'After all, no sane man would believe in witches and warlocks and sabbaths and spells and all that tarradiddle. No, I merely collect them as interesting books which are of value and in many cases, because of their contents, exceedingly amusing.'

'Amusing?' he said, coming forward to accept the glass of wine I held out to him. 'How do you mean, amusing?'

'Well, don't you find amusing the thought of grown men mumbling all those silly spells and standing about for hours in the middle of the night expecting Satan to appear? I confess I find it very amusing indeed.'

'I do not,' he said, and then, as if he feared that he had been too abrupt and perhaps rude, he smiled and raised his glass. 'Your very good health, Mr Letting.'

We drank. He rolled the wine round his mouth and then raised his eyebrows.

'May I compliment you on your cellar,' he said. 'This is an excellent Margaux.'

'Thank you,' I said, flattered, I must confess, that this aristocratic Frenchman should approve my choice in wine. 'Won't you have a chair and perhaps explain to me how I may be of service to you.'

He seated himself elegantly in a chair by the fire, sipped his

146

wine and stared at me thoughtfully for a moment. When his face was in repose you noticed the size and blackness and lustre of his eyes. They seem to probe you, almost as if they could read your very thoughts. The impression they gave made me uncomfortable, to say the least. But then he smiled and immediately the eyes flashed with mischief, good humour and an overwhelming charm.

'I'm afraid that my unexpected arrival so late at night . . . and on such a night . . . must lend an air of mystery to what is, I'm afraid, a very ordinary request that I have to make of you. Simply, it is that I should like you to catalogue a library for me, a comparatively small collection of books, not above twelve hundred I surmise, which was left to me by my aunt when she died last year. As I say, it is only a small collection of books and I have done no more than give it a cursory glance. However, I believe it to contain some quite rare and valuable things and I feel it necessary to have it properly catalogued, a precaution my aunt never took, poor dear. She was a woman with a mind of cotton wool and never, I dare swear, opened a book from the start of her life until the end of it. She led an existence untrammelled and unruffled by the slightest breeze of culture. She had inherited the books from her father and from the day they came into her possession she never paid them the slightest regard. They are a muddled and confused mess, and I would be grateful if you would lend me your expertise in sorting them out. The reason that I have invaded your house at such an hour is force of circumstances, for I must go back to France tomorrow morning very early, and this was my only chance of seeing you. I do hope you can spare the time to do this for me?'

'I shall be happy to be of what assistance I can,' I said, for I must admit that the idea of a trip to France was a pleasant thought, 'but I am curious to know why you have picked on me when there are so many people in Paris who could do the job just as well, if not better.'

'I think you do yourself an injustice,' said my visitor. 'You must be aware of the excellent reputation you enjoy. I asked a number of people for their advice and when I found that they all spontaneously advised me to ask you, then I was sure that, if you agreed to do the work, I would be getting the very best, my dear Mr Letting.'

I confess I flushed with pleasure, since I had no reason to doubt the man's sincerity. It was pleasant to know that my colleagues thought so highly of me.

'When would you wish me to commence?' I asked.

He spread his hands and gave an expressive shrug.

'I'm in no hurry,' he said. 'Naturally I would have to fall in with your plans. But I was wondering if, say, you could start some time in the spring? The Loire valley is particularly beautiful then and there is no reason why you should not enjoy the countryside as well as catalogue books.'

'The spring would suit me admirably,' I said, pouring out some more wine. 'Would April be all right?'

'Excellent,' he said. 'I would think that the job would take you a month or so, but from my point of view please stay as long as it is necessary. I have a good cellar and a good chef, so I can minister to the wants of the flesh at any rate.'

I fetched my diary and we settled on April the fourteenth as being a suitable date for both of us. My visitor rose to go.

'Just one other thing,' he said as he swirled his cloak around his shoulders. 'I would be the first to admit that I have a difficult name both to remember and to pronounce. Therefore, if you would not consider it presumptuous of me, I would like you to call me Gideon and may I call you Peter?'

'Of course,' I said immediately and with some relief, for the name de Teildras Villeray was not one that slid easily off the tongue.

He shook my hand warmly, once again apologized for disturbing me, promised he would write with full details of how to reach him in France and then strode off confidently into the swirling yellow fog and was soon lost to view.

I returned to my warm and comfortable drawing-room and finished the bottle of wine while musing on my strange visitor. The more I thought about it the more curious the whole incident became. For example, why had Gideon not approached me when he first saw me at Sotheby's? He said that he was in no hurry to have his library catalogued and yet felt it imperative that he should see me, late at night, as if the matter was of great urgency. Surely he could have written to me? Or did he perhaps think that the force of his personality would make me accept a commission that I might otherwise refuse?

I was in two minds about the man himself. As I said, when his face was in repose his eyes were so fiercely brooding and penetrating that they made me uneasy and filled almost with a sense of repugnance. But then when he smiled and his eyes filled with laughter and he talked with that husky, musical voice, I had been charmed in spite of myself. He was, I decided, a very curious character, and I determined that I would try to find out more about him before I went over to France. Having made this resolution, I made my way down to the kitchen, preceded by a now hungry Neptune, and cooked myself a late supper.

A few days later I ran into my old friend Edward Mallenger at a sale. During the course of it I asked him casually if he knew of Gideon. He gave me a very penetrating look from over the top of his glasses.

'Gideon de Teildras Villeray?' he asked. 'D'you mean the Count . . . the nephew of the old Marquis de Teildras Villeray?'

'He didn't tell me he was a Count, but I suppose it must be the same one,' I said. 'Do you know anything about him?'

'When the sale is over we'll go and have a drink and I'll tell you,' said Edward. 'They are a very odd family . . . at least, the old Marquis is distinctly odd.'

The sale over we repaired to the local pub and over a drink Edward told me what he knew of Gideon. It appeared that, many years previously, the Marquis de Teildras Villeray had asked my friend to go to France (just as Gideon had done with me) to catalogue and value his extensive library. Edward had accepted the commission and had set off for the Marquis's place in the Gorge du Tarn.

'Do you know that area of France?' Edward asked.

'I have never been to France at all,' I confessed.

'Well, it's a desolate area. The house is in a wild and remote district right in the Gorge itself. It's a rugged country, with huge cliffs and deep gloomy gorges, waterfalls and rushing torrents, not unlike the Gustave Doré drawings for Dante's Inferno, you know.'

Edward paused to sip his drink thoughtfully, and then occupied himself with lighting a cigar. When it was drawing to his satisfaction, he went on. 'In the house, apart from the family retainers of which there only seemed to be three (a small number for such a large establishment) was the uncle and his nephew whom, I take it, was your visitor of the other night. The uncle was – well, not to put too fine a point on it, a most unpleasant old man. He must have been about eighty-five, I suppose, with a really evil, leering face, and an oily manner that he obviously thought was charming. The boy was about fourteen with huge dark eyes in a pale face. He was an intelligent lad, old for his age, but the thing that worried me was that he seemed to be suffering from intense fear, a fear, I felt, of his uncle.

'The first night I arrived, after we had had dinner, which was, to my mind meagre and badly-cooked fare for France, I went to bed early, for I was fatigued after my journey. The old man and the boy stayed up. As luck would have it the dining-room was directly below my bedroom, and so, although I could not hear clearly all that passed between them I could hear enough to discern that the old man was doing his best to persuade his nephew into some course of action that the boy found repugnant, for he was vehement in his refusal. The argument went on for some time, the uncle's voice getting louder and louder and more angry. Suddenly, I heard the scrape of a chair as the boy stood and shouted, positively shouted, my dear Peter – in French at his uncle: "No, no, I will not be devoured so that you may live . . . I hate you." I heard it quite clearly and I thought it an astonishing thing for a young boy to say. Then I heard the door of the dining-salon open and bang shut, the boy's footsteps running up stairs and, eventually, the banging of what I assumed was his bedroom door.

'After a short while I heard the uncle get up from the table and start to come upstairs. There was no mistaking his footfall, for one of his feet was twisted and misshapen and so he walked slowly with a pronounced limp, dragging his left foot. He came slowly up the stairs, and I do assure you, my dear Peter, there was positive evil in this slow, shuffling approach that really made my hair stand on end. I heard him go to the boy's bedroom door, open it and enter. He called the boy's name two or three times, softly and cajolingly, but with indescribable menace. Then he said one sentence which I could not catch. After this he closed the boy's door and for some moments I could hear him dragging and shuffling down the long corridor to his own quarters.

'I opened my door and from the boy's room I could hear muffled weeping, as though the poor child had his head under the bedclothes. It went on for a long time, and I was very worried. I wanted to go and comfort the lad, but I felt it might embarrass him, and in any case it was really none of my business. But I did not like the situation at all. The whole atmosphere, my dear Peter, was charged with something unpleasant.

'I am not a superstitious man, as you well know, but I lay awake for a long time and wondered if I could stay in the atmosphere of that house for the two or three weeks it would take me to finish the job which I had agreed to do. Fortunately, fate gave me the chance I needed: the very next day I received a telegram to say that my sister had fallen gravely ill and so, quite legitimately, I could ask de Teildras Villeray to release me from my contract. He was, of course, most reluctant to do so, but he eventually agreed with ill-grace.

'While I was waiting for the dog cart to arrive to take me to the station, I had a quick look round some of his library. Since it was really extensive it spread all over the house, but the bulk of it was housed in what he referred to as the Long Gallery, a very handsome, long room, that would not have disgraced one of our aristocratic country houses. It was hung with giant mirrors between the bookcases, in fact, the whole house was full of mirrors. I can never remember being in a house with so many before.

'He certainly had a rare and valuable collection of books, particularly on one of your pet subjects, Peter, the occult. I noticed, in my hurried browse, among other things, some most interesting Hebrew manuscripts on witchcraft, as well as an original of Matthew Hopkin's *Discovery of Witches* and a truly beautiful copy of Dee's *De Mirabilius Naturae*. But then the dog cart arrived and, making my farewells, I left.

'I can tell you, my dear boy, I was never so glad in my life to be quit of a house. I truly believe the old man to have been evil and would not be surprised to learn that he practised witchcraft and was trying to involve that nice young lad in his foul affairs. However, I have no proof of this, you understand, so that is why I would not wish to repeat it. I should imagine that the uncle is now dead, or, if not, he must be in his nineties. As to the boy, I later heard from friends in Paris that there were rumours that his private life was not all that it should be, some talk of his attachment to certain women, you know, but this was all circumstantial, and in any case, as you know dear boy, foreigners have a different set of morals to an Englishman. It is one of the many things that sets us apart from the rest of the world, thank God.'

I had listened with great interest to Edward's account, and I resolved to ask Gideon about his uncle if I got the chance.

I prepared myself for my trip to France with, I must admit, pleasurable anticipation, and on April the fourteenth I embarked on the train to Dover and thence, uneventfully (even to *mal de mer*), to Calais. I spent the night in Paris, sampling the delights of French food and wine, and the following day I embarked once more on the train. Eventually I arrived at the bustling station at Tours. Gideon was there to meet me as he had promised he would. He seemed in great spirits and greeted me as if I was an old and valued friend, which, I confess, flattered me. I thanked him for coming to meet me, but he waved my thanks away.

'It's nothing, my dear Peter.' he said. 'I have nothing to do except eat, drink and grow fat. A visit from someone like you is a rare pleasure.'

Outside the station we entered a handsome brougham drawn by two beautiful bay horses and we set off at a spanking pace through the most delicious countryside, all green and gold and shimmering in the sunlight.

We drove for an hour along roads that got progressively narrower and narrower, until we were travelling along between high banks emblazoned with flowers of every sort, while overhead, the branches of the trees on each side of the road entwined, covered with the delicate green leaves of spring. Occasionally there would be a gap in the trees and high banks and I would see the silver gleam of the Loire between the trees. I realized that we were driving parallel to the great river. Once we passed the massive stone gateposts and wrought-iron gates that guarded the drive up to an immense and very beautiful château in gleaming pinky-yellow stone. Gideon saw me looking at it, perhaps with an expression of wonder, for it did look like something out of a fairy tale. He smiled.

'I hope, my dear Peter, that you do not expect to find me living in a monster like that? If so, you will be doomed to disappointment. I am afraid that my château is a miniature one, but big enough for my needs.'

I protested that I did not care if he lived in a cow shed: for me the experience of being in France for the first time and seeing all these new sights and with the prospect of a fascinating job at the end of it, was more than sufficient.

It was not until evening, when the mauve tree shadows were stretched long across the green meadows, that we came to Gideon's establishment, the Château St Claire. The gateposts were surmounted by two large, delicately carved owls in a pale honey-coloured stone, and I saw that the same motif had been carried out most skilfully in the wrought-iron gates that hung from the pillars.

As soon as we entered the grounds I was struck by the contrast to the countryside we had been passing through, which had been exuberant and unkempt, alive with wild flowers and meadows, shaggy with long rich grass. Here the drive was lined with giant oak and chestnut trees, each the circumference of a small room, gnarled and ancient, with bark as thick as an elephant's hide. How many hundred years these trees had guarded the entrance to the Château St Claire, I could not imagine, but many of them must have been well-grown when Shakespeare was a young man. The green sward under them was as smooth as baize on a billiard table, and responsible for this, were several herds of spotted fallow deer, grazing peacefully in the setting sun's rays. The bucks, with their fine twisted antlers, threw up their heads and gazed at us without fear as we clopped past them and down the avenue.

Beyond the green sward I could see a line of gigantic poplars and, gleaming between them, the Loire. Then the drive turned away from the river and the château came into sight. It was, as Gideon had said, small but perfect, as a miniature is perfect. In the evening sun its pale straw-coloured walls glowed and the light gave a soft and delicate patina to the blueish slate of the roofs of the main house and its two turrets.

It was surrounded by a wide veranda of great flag stone,

hemmed in by a wide balustrade on which were perched above thirty peacocks, their magnificent tails trailing down towards the well-kept lawn. Around the balustrade, the flower beds, beautifully kept, were ablaze with flowers in a hundred different colours that seemed to merge with the tails of the peacocks that trailed amongst them. It was a breathtaking sight. The carriage pulled up by the wide steps, the butler threw open the door of the brougham, and Gideon dismounted, took off his hat and swept me a low bow, grinning mischievously.

'Welcome to the Château St Claire,' he said.

Thus for me began an enchanted three weeks, for it was more of a holiday than work. The miniature, but impeccably kept and furnished château was a joy to live in. The tiny park that meandered along the river bank was also beautifully kept, for every tree looked as if it were freshly groomed, the emerald lawns combed each morning, and the peacocks, trailing their glittering tails amongst the massive trees, as if they had just left the careful hands of Fabergé. Combine this with a fine cellar and a kitchen ruled over by a red balloon of a chef whose deft hands would conjure up the most delicate and aromatic of meals, and you had a close approach to an earthly paradise.

The morning would be spent sorting and cataloguing the books (and a most interesting collection it was) and then in the afternoon Gideon would insist that we went swimming or else for a ride round the park, for he possessed a small stable of very nice horses. In the evenings, after dinner, we would sit on the still sun-warmed terrace and talk, our conversation made warm and friendly by the wine we had consumed and the excellent meal we had eaten.

Gideon was an excellent host, a brilliant raconteur and this, together with his extraordinary gift for mimicry, made him a most entertaining companion. I shall never know now, of course, whether he deliberately exerted all his charm in order to ensnare me. I like to think not; that he quite genuinely liked me and my company. Not that I suppose it matters now. But certainly, as day followed day, I grew fonder and fonder of Gideon.

I am a solitary creature by nature, and I have only a very small circle of friends – close friends – whom I see perhaps once or twice a year, preferring, for the most part, my own company. However, my time spent at the château with Gideon had an extraordinary effect upon me. It began to dawn upon me that I had perhaps made myself into too much of a recluse. It was also borne upon me most forcibly that all my friends were of a different age group, much older than I was. Gideon, if I could count him as a friend (and by this time I certainly did), was the only friend I had who was, roughly speaking, my own age. Under his influence I began to expand. As he said to me one night, a slim cigar crushed between his strong white teeth, squinting at me past the blue smoke, 'the trouble with you, Peter, is that you are in danger of becoming a young fogey'. I laughed, of course, but on reflection I knew he was right. I also knew that when the time came for me to leave the château I would miss his volatile company a great deal, probably more than I cared to admit, even to myself.

In all our talks Gideon discussed his extensive family with a sort of ironic affection, telling me anecdotes to illustrate their stupidity or their eccentricity, never maliciously but rather with a sort of detached good humour. However, the curious thing was that he never once mentioned his uncle, the Marquis, until one evening. We were sitting out on the terrace, watching the white owls that lived in the hollow oaks along the drive doing their first hunting swoops across the green sward in front of us. I had been telling him of a book which I knew was to be put up for sale in the autumn and which I thought could be purchased for some two thousand pounds. It was an important work and I felt he should have it in his library as it complemented the other works he had on the subject. Did he want me to bid for him? He flipped his cigar butt over the balustrade into the flower bed where it lay gleaming like a monstrous red glow worm, and chuckled softly.

'Two thousand pounds?' he said. 'My dear Peter, I am not rich enough to indulge my hobby to that extent, unfortunately. If my uncle were to die now it would be a different story.'

'Your uncle?' I queried cautiously. 'I did not know you had any uncles.'

'Only one, thank God,' said Gideon, 'but unfortunately he holds the purse strings of the family fortunes and the old swine appears to be indestructible. He is ninety-one and when I last saw him, a year or two back, he did not look a day over fifty. However, in spite of all his efforts I do not believe him to be immortal and so one day the devil will gather him to his bosom. On that happy day I will inherit a very large sum of money and a library that will make even you, my dear Peter, envious. Until that day comes I cannot go around spending two thousand pounds on a book. But waiting for dead men's shoes is a tedious occupation, and my uncle is an unsavoury topic of conversation, so let's have some more wine and talk of something pleasant.'

'If he is unsavoury, then he is in contrast to the rest of your relatives you have told me about,' I said lightly, hoping that he would give me further information about his infamous uncle.

Gideon was silent for a moment.

'Yes, a great contrast,' he said, 'but as every village must have its idiot, so every family must have its black sheep or its madman.'

'Oh, come now, Gideon,' I protested. 'Surely that's a bit too harsh a criticism?'

'You think so?' he asked and in the half light I could see that his face was shining with sweat. 'You think I am being harsh to my dear relative? But then you have not had the pleasure of meeting him, have you?'

'No,' I said, worried by the savage bitterness in his voice and wishing that I had let the subject drop since it seemed to disturb him so much.

'When my mother died I had to go and live with my dear uncle for several years until I inherited the modest amount of money my father left me in trust and I could be free of him. For ten years I lived in purgatory with that corrupt old swine. For ten years not a day or a night passed without my being terrified out of my soul. There are no words to describe how evil he is, and there are no lengths to which he will not go to achieve his ends. If Satan prowls the earth in the guise of a man then he surely inhabits the filthy skin of my uncle.'

He got up abruptly and went into the house. I was puzzled and alarmed at the vehemence with which he had spoken. I did not know whether to follow him or not, but presently he returned carrying the brandy decanter and two glasses. He sat down and poured us both a generous amount of the spirit.

'I must apologize, my dear Peter, for all my histrionics, for inflicting you with melodrama that would be more in keeping in the *Grande Guignol* than on this terrace,' he said, handing me my drink. 'Talking of my old swine of an uncle has that effect on me, I'm afraid. At one time I lived in fear because I thought he had captured my soul . . . you know the stupid ideas children get? It was many years before I grew out of that. But it still, as you can see, upsets me to talk of him, so let's drink and talk of other things, eh?'

I agreed wholeheartedly, and we talked pleasantly for a couple of hours or so. But that night was the only time I saw Gideon go to bed the worse for liquor. I felt most guilty since I felt it was due to my insistence that he talk about his uncle who had made such a deep, lasting and unpleasant impression on his mind.

Over the next four years I grew to know Gideon well. He came to stay with me whenever he was in England and I paid several delightful visits to the Château St Claire. Then for a period of six months I heard nothing from him. I could only presume that he had been overcome by what he called his 'travel disease' and had gone off to Egypt or the Far East or even America on one of his periodic jaunts. However, this coincided with a time when I was, myself, extremely busy and so I had little time to ponder on the whereabouts of Gideon. Then, one evening, I returned home to Smith Street dead tired after a long journey from Aberdeen and I found awaiting me a telegram from Gideon.

Arriving London Monday thirty can I stay stop Uncle put to death I inherit library would you catalogue value move stop explain all when we meet regards Gideon.

I was amused that Gideon, who prided himself on his impeccable English, should have written 'put to death' instead of 'died' until he arrived and I discovered that this is exactly what had happened to his uncle, or, at least, what appeared to have happened. Gideon arrived quite late on the Monday evening and as soon as I looked at him I could see that he had been undergoing some harrowing experience. Surely, I thought to myself, it could not be the death of his uncle that was affecting him so. If anything I would have thought he would have been glad. But my friend had lost weight, his handsome face was gaunt and white and he had dark circles under his eyes that seemed suddenly to have lost all their sparkle and lustre. When I poured him out a glass of his favourite wine he took it with a hand that trembled slightly and tossed it back in one gulp as if it had been mere water.

'You look tired, Gideon,' I said. 'You must have a few glasses of wine and then I suggest an early dinner and bed. We can discuss all there is to be discussed in the morning.'

'Dear old Peter,' he said, giving me a shadow of his normally effervescent smile. 'Please don't act like an English nanny, and take that worried look off your face. I am not sickening for anything. It's just that I have had rather a hard time these last few weeks and I'm suffering from reaction. However, it's all over now, thank God. I'll tell you all about it over dinner, but before then I would be grateful if I could have a bath, my dear chap.'

'Of course,' I said immediately, and went to ask Mrs Manning to draw a bath for my friend, and to take his baggage up to the guest room.

He went upstairs to bathe and change, and very shortly I followed him. Both my bedroom and the guest room had their own bathrooms, for there was sufficient room on that floor to allow this little luxury. I was just about to start undressing in order to start my own ablutions when I was startled by a loud moaning cry, almost a strangled scream, followed by a crash of breaking glass which appeared to emanate from Gideon's bathroom. I hastened across the narrow landing and tapped on his door.

'Gideon?' I called. 'Gideon, are you all right . . . can I come in?'

There was no reply and so, greatly agitated, I entered the room. I found my friend in his bathroom, bent over the basin and holding on to it for support, his face the ghastly white of cheese, sweat streaming down it. The big mirror over the basin had been shattered and the fragments, together with a broken bottle of what looked like hair shampoo, littered the basin and the floor around.

'He did it . . . he did it . . . he did it . . .' muttered Gideon to himself, swaying, clutching hold of the basin. He seemed oblivious of my presence. I seized him by the arm and helped him into the bedroom where I made him lie down on the bed and called down the stairs for Mrs Manning to bring up some brandy and look sharp about it.

When I went back into the room Gideon was looking a little better, but he was lying there with his eyes closed, taking deep, shuddering breaths like a man who has just run a gruelling race. When he heard me approach the bed he opened his eyes and gave me a ghastly smile.

'My dear Peter,' he said, 'I do apologize . . . so stupid of me
. . . I suddenly felt faint . . . I think it must be the journey and
lack of food, plus your excellent wine . . . I fear I fell forward
with that bottle in my hand and shattered your beautiful
mirror . . . I'm so sorry . . . of course I will replace it.'

I told him, quite brusquely, not to be so silly and, when Mrs
Manning came panting up the stairs with the brandy, I forced
him to take some in spite of his protests. While he was drinking
it, Mrs Manning cleaned up the mess in the bathroom.

'Ah. That's better,' said Gideon at last. 'I feel quite revived
now. All I want is a nice relaxing bath and I shall be a new
man.'

I felt that he ought to have his food in bed, but he would not
hear of it, and when he descended to the dining-room half an
hour later I must say he did look better and much more
relaxed. He laughed and joked with Mrs Manning as she served
us and complimented her lavishly on her cooking, swearing that
he would get rid of his own chef, kidnap Mrs Manning and take
her to his château in France to cook for him. Mrs Manning was
enchanted by him, as indeed she always was, but I could see
that it cost him some effort to be so charming and jovial. When
at last we had finished the pudding and cheese and Mrs Manning put the decanter of port on the table and saying good
night, left us, Gideon accepted a cigar. Having lit it he leant
back in his chair and smiled at me through the smoke.

'Now, Peter,' he began, 'I can tell you something of what's
been happening.'

'I am most anxious to know what it is that has brought you to
this low ebb, my friend,' I said seriously.

He felt in his pocket and produced from it a large iron key
with heavy teeth and an ornate butt. He threw it on the table
where it fell with a heavy thud.

'This was one of the causes of the trouble,' he said, staring
at it moodily. 'The key to life and death, as you might say.'

'I don't understand you,' I said, puzzled.

'Because of this key I was nearly arrested for murder,' said Gideon, with a smile.

'Murder? You?' I exclaimed, aghast. 'But how can that possibly be?'

Gideon took a sip at his glass of port and settled himself back in his chair.

'About two months ago I got a letter from my uncle asking me to go to see him. This I did, with considerable reluctance as you may imagine for you know what my opinion of him was. Well, to cut a long story short, there were certain things he wanted me to do . . . er . . . family matters . . . which I refused to do. He flew into a rage and we quarrelled furiously. I am afraid that I left him in no doubt as to what I thought of him and the servants heard us quarrel. I left his house and continued on my way to Marseilles to catch a boat for Morocco where I was going for a tour. Two days later my uncle was murdered.'

'So that's why you put "uncle put to death" in your telegram,' I said. ' I wondered.'

'He *had* been put to death, and in the most mysterious circumstances,' said Gideon. 'He was found in an empty attic at the top of the house which contained nothing but a large broken mirror. He was a hideous mess, his clothes torn off him, his throat and body savaged as if by a mad dog. There was blood everywhere. I had to identify the body. It was not a pleasant task, for his face had been so badly mauled that it was almost unrecognizable.' He paused and took another sip of port. Presently he went on. 'But the curious thing about all this was that the attic was locked, *locked on the inside* with that key.'

'But how could that be?' I asked, bewildered. 'How did his assailant leave the room?'

'That's exactly what the police wanted to know,' said Gideon dryly. 'As you know the French police are very efficient but lacking in imagination. Their logic worked something like this: I was the one that stood to gain by my uncle's death because I inherit the family fortune and his library and several farms dotted about all over France. So, as I was the one that stood to gain, *enfin*, I must be the one who committed murder.'

'But that's ridiculous,' I broke in indignantly.

'Not to a policeman,' said Gideon, 'especially when they heard that at my last meeting with my uncle we had quarrelled bitterly and one of the things that the servants heard me saying to him was that I wished he would drop dead and thus leave the world a cleaner place.'

'But in the heat of a quarrel one is liable to say anything,' I protested. 'Everyone knows that . . . And how did they suggest you killed your uncle and then left the room locked on the inside?'

'Oh, it was possible, quite possible,' said Gideon. 'With a pair of long-nosed, very slender pliers, it could have been done, but it would undoubtedly have left marks on the end of the key, and as you can see it's unmarked. The real problem was that at first I had no alibi. I had gone down to Marseilles and, as I had cut my visit to my uncle short, I was too early for my ship. I booked into a small hotel and enjoyed myself for those few days in exploring the port. I knew no one there so, naturally, there was no one to vouch for my movements. As you can imagine, it took time to assemble all the porters, maids, *maîtres d'hôtel*, restaurant owners, hotel managers and so on, and through their testimony prove to the police that I was, in fact, in Marseilles and minding my own business when my uncle was killed. It has taken me the last six weeks to do it, and it has been extremely exhausting.'

'Why didn't you telegraph me?' I asked. 'I could have come and at least kept you company.'

'You are very kind, Peter, but I did not want to embroil my friends in such a sordid mess. Besides, I knew that if all went well and the police released me (which they eventually did after much protest) I should want your help on something appertaining to this.'

'Anything I can do,' I said. 'You know you have only to ask,

163

my dear fellow.'

'Well, as I told you I spent my youth under my uncle's care, and after that experience I grew to loathe his house and everything about it. Now, with this latest thing, I really feel I cannot set foot in the place again. I am not exaggerating but I seriously think that if I were to go there and stay I should become seriously ill.'

'I agree,' I said firmly. 'On no account must you even contemplate such a step.'

'Well, the furniture and the house I can of course get valued and sold by a Paris firm: that is simple. But the most valuable thing in the house is the library. This is where you come in, Peter. Would you be willing to go down and catalogue and value the books for me. Then I can arrange for them to be stored until I can build an extension to my library to house them?'

'Of course I will,' I said. 'With the greatest of pleasure. You just tell me when you want me to come.'

'I shall not be with you, you'll be quite alone,' Gideon warned.

'I am a solitary creature, as I have told you,' I laughed, 'and as long as I have a supply of books to amuse me I shall get along splendidly, don't worry.'

'I would like it done as soon as possible,' said Gideon, 'so that I may get rid of the house. How soon could you come down?'

I consulted my diary and found that, fortunately, I was coming up to a rather slack period.

'How about the end of next week?' I asked and Gideon's face lit up.

'So soon?' he said delightedly. 'That would be splendid! I could meet you at the station at Fontaine next Friday. Would that be all right?'

'Perfectly all right,' I said, 'and I will soon have the books sorted out for you. Now, another glass of port and then you must away to bed.'

'My dear Peter, what a loss you are to Harley Street,' joked Gideon, but he took my advice.

Twice during the night I awakened, thinking that I heard him cry out but, after listening for a while all was quiet and I concluded that it was just my imagination. The following morning he left for France and I started making my preparations to follow him, packing sufficient things for a prolonged stay at his late uncle's house.

The whole of Europe was in the grip of an icy winter and it was certainly not the weather to travel in. Indeed no one but Gideon could have got me to leave home in such weather. Crossing the Channel was a nightmare and I felt so sick on arrival in Paris that I could not do more than swallow a little broth and go straight to bed. The following day it was icy cold, with a bitter wind, grey skies and driving veils of rain that stung your face. Eventually I reached the station and boarded the train for what seemed an interminable journey, during which I had to change and wait at more and more inhospitable stations, until I was so numbed with cold I could hardly think straight. All the rivers wore a rim of lacy ice along their shores, and the ponds and lakes turned blank, frozen eyes to the steel grey sky.

At length, the local train I had changed to dragged itself, grimy and puffing, into the station of Fontaine. I disembarked and made my way with my luggage to the tiny booking office and minute waiting-room. Here, to my relief I found that there was an old-fashioned, pot-bellied stove stuffed with chestnut roots and glowing almost red hot. I piled my luggage in the corner and spent some time thawing myself out, for the heating on the train had been minimal. There was no sign of Gideon. Presently, warmed by the fire and a nip of brandy, I had taken from my travelling flask, I began to feel better. Half an hour passed and I began to worry about Gideon's absence. I went out on to the platform and discovered that the grey sky seemed to have moved closer to the earth and a few snowflakes were starting to fall, huge lacy ones the size of a half crown, that augured a snowstorm of considerable dimensions in the not too distant future. I was just wondering if I should try walking to the village when I heard the clop of hooves and made out a dog cart coming along the road driven by Gideon muffled up in a glossy fur coat and wearing an astrakhan hat.

'I'm so very sorry, Peter, for keeping you waiting like this,' he said, wringing my hand, 'but we seem to have one catastrophe after another. Come, let me help you with your bags and I will tell you all about it as we drive.'

We collected my baggage, bundled it into the dog cart and then I climbed up on to the box alongside Gideon and covered myself thankfully with the thick fur rug he had brought. He turned the horse, cracked his whip and we went, bowling down the snowflakes which were now falling quite fast. The wind whipped our faces and made our eyes water, but still Gideon kept the horse at a fast trot.

'I am anxious to get there before the snowstorm really starts,' he said, 'that is why I am going at this uncivilized pace. Once these snowstorms start up here they can be very severe. One can get snowed in for days at a time.'

'It is certainly becoming a grim winter,' I said.

'The worst we've had here for fifty years,' said Gideon.

We came to the village and Gideon was silent as he guided his horse through the narrow, deserted streets, already white with settling snow. Occasionally a dog would run out of an alley and run barking alongside us for a way, but otherwise there was no sign of life. The village could have been deserted for all evidence to the contrary.

'I am afraid that once again, my dear Peter, I shall have to trespass upon your good nature,' said Gideon, smiling at me, his hat and his eyebrows white with snow. 'Sooner or later my demands on our friendship will exhaust your patience.'

'Nonsense,' I said, 'just tell me what the problem is.'

'Well,' said Gideon, 'I was to leave you in the charge of

François and his wife, who were my uncle's servants. Unfortunately, when I went to the house this morning I found that François's wife Marie, had slipped on the icy front steps and had fallen some thirty feet on to the rocks and broken her legs. They are, I'm afraid, splintered very badly, and I don't hold out much hope for them being saved.'

'Poor woman, how dreadful,' I exclaimed.

'Yes,' Gideon continued. 'Of course François was nearly frantic when I got there, and so there was nothing for it but to drive them both to the hospital in Milau which took me over two hours, hence my being so late meeting you.'

'That doesn't matter at all,' I said. 'Of course you had to drive them to the hospital.'

'Yes, but it created another problem as well,' said Gideon. 'You see, none of the villagers liked my uncle, and François and Marie were the only couple who would work for him. With both of them in Milau, there is no one to look after you, at least for two or three days until François comes back.'

'My dear chap, don't let that worry you,' I laughed. 'I am quite used to fending for myself, I do assure you. If I have food and wine and a fire I will be very well found I promise you.'

'Oh, you'll have all that,' said Gideon. 'The larder is well stocked, and down in the game room there is a haunch of venison, half a wild boar, some pheasants and partridge and a few brace of wild duck. There is wine aplenty, since my uncle kept quite a good cellar, and the cellar is full of chestnut roots and pine logs, so you will be warm. You will also have for company the animals.'

'Animals, what animals?' I asked, curious.

'A small dog called Agrippa,' said Gideon, laughing, 'a very large and idiotic cat called Clair de Lune, or Clair for short, a whole cage of canaries and various finches and an extremely old parrot called Octavius.'

'A positive menagerie,' I exclaimed. 'It's a good thing that I like animals.'

'Seriously, Peter,' asked Gideon, giving me one of his very penetrating looks, 'are you sure you will be all right? It seems a terrible imposition to me.'

'Nonsense,' I said heartily, 'what are friends for?'

The snow was coming down with a vengeance and we could only see a yard or two beyond the horse's ears, so dense were the whirling clouds of huge flakes. We had now entered one of the many tributary gorges that led into the Gorge du Tarn proper. On our left the brown and black cliffs, dappled with patches of snow on sundry crevices and ledges, loomed over us, in places actually overhanging the narrow road. On our right the ground dropped away, almost sheer, five or six hundred feet into the gorge below where, through the wind-blown curtains of snow, one could catch occasional glimpses of the green river, its tumbled rocks snow-wigged, their edges crusted with ice. The road was rough, snow and water worn, and in places covered with a sheet of ice which made the horse slip and stumble and slowed our progress. Once a small avalanche of snow slid down the cliff face with a hissing sound and thumped on to the road in front of us, making the horse shy so badly that Gideon had to fight to keep control. For several hair-raising minutes I feared that we, the dog cart and the terrified horse might slide over the edge of the gorge and plunge down into the river below. But eventually Gideon got it under control and we crawled along our way.

Eventually the gorge widened a little and presently we rounded a corner and there before us was the strange bulk of Gideon's uncle's house. It was an extraordinary edifice and I feel I should describe it in some detail. To begin with the whole thing was perched on top of a massive rock that protruded from the river far below so that it formed what could only be described as an island, shaped not unlike an isosceles triangle, with the house on top. It was connected to the road by a massive and very old stone bridge. The tall outside walls of the house fell sheer down to the rocks and river below, but as you crossed the bridge and drove under a huge arch, guarded by thick oak doors, you found that the house was built round a large centre courtyard, cobblestoned and with a pond with a fountain in the middle. This depicted a dolphin held up by cherubs, the whole thing polished with ice, and with icicles hanging from it.

All the many windows that looked down into the court were shuttered with a fringe of huge icicles hanging from every cornice. Between the windows were monstrous gargoyles depicting various forms of animal life, known and unknown to science, each one seeming more malign than the last and their appearance not improved by the ice and snow that blurred their outlines so that they seemed to be peering at you from snowy ambush. As Gideon drew the horse to a standstill by the steps that led to the front door we could hear the barking of the dog inside. My friend opened the front door with a large, rusty key and immediately the dog tumbled out, barking vociferously and wagging its tail with pleasure. The large black and white cat was more circumspect and did not deign to come out into the snow, but merely stood, arching its back and mewing in the doorway. Gideon helped me carry my bags into the large marble hall where a handsome staircase led to the upper floors of the house. All the pictures, mirrors and furniture were covered with dust sheets.

'I am sorry about the covers,' said Gideon. It seemed to me that, as soon as he had entered the house, he had become nervous and ill at ease. 'I meant to remove them all this morning and make it more habitable for you, but what with one thing and another I did not manage it.'

'Don't worry,' I said, making a fuss of the dog and cat, who were both vying for my attention. 'I shan't be inhabiting all the house, so I will just remove the sheets in those parts that I shall use.'

'Yes, yes,' said Gideon, running his hands through his hair in a nervous fashion. 'Your bed is made up . . . the bedroom is the second door on the left as you reach the top of the stairs.

Now, come with me and I'll show you the kitchen and cellar.'

He led me across the hall to a door that was hidden under the main staircase. Opening this he made his way down broad stone steps that spiralled their way down into the gloom. Presently we reached a passageway that led to a gigantic stone-flagged kitchen and, adjoining it, cavernous cellars and a capacious larder, cold as a glacier, with the carcases of game, chicken, duck, legs of lamb and saddles of beef hanging from hooks or lying on the marble shelves that ran around the walls. In the kitchen was a great range, each fire carefully laid, and on the huge table in the centre had been arranged various commodities that Gideon thought I might need, rice, lentils as black as soot, potatoes, carrots and other vegetables in large baskets, pottery jars of butter and conserves, and a pile of freshly-baked loaves. On the opposite side of the kitchen to the cellars and larder lay the wine store, approached through a heavy door, bolted and padlocked. Obviously Gideon's uncle had not trusted his staff when it came to alcoholic beverages. The cellar was small, but I saw at a glance it contained some excellent vintages.

'Do not stint yourself, Peter,' said Gideon. 'There are some really quite nice wines in there and they will be some small compensation for staying in the gloomy place alone.'

'You want me to spend my time in an inebriated state?' I laughed. 'I would never get the books valued. But don't worry Gideon, I shall be quite all right. I have food and wine enough for an army, plenty of fuel for the fire, a dog and a cat and birds to bear me company and a large and interesting library. What more could any man want?'

'The books, by the way, are mainly in the Long Gallery, on the south side of the house. I won't show it to you . . . it's easy enough to find, and I really must be on my way,' said Gideon, leading the way up into the hall once more. He delved into his pocket and produced a huge bunch of ancient keys. 'The keys of the kingdom,' he said with a faint smile. 'I don't think anything is locked, but if it is, please open it. I will tell François that he is to come back here and look after you as soon as his wife is out of danger, and I, myself, will return in about four weeks' time. By then you should have finished your task.'

'Easily,' I said. 'In fact, if I get it done before then I will send you a telegram.'

'Seriously, Peter,' he said, taking my hand, 'I am really most deeply in your debt for what you are doing. I shall not forget it.'

'Rubbish, my friend,' I said. 'It gives me great pleasure to be of service to you.'

I stood in the doorway of the house, the dog panting by my side, the cat arching itself around my legs and purring loudly, and watched Gideon get back into the dog cart, wrap the rug around himself and then flick the horses with the reins. As they broke into a trot and he steered them towards the entrance to the courtyard he raised his whip in salute. He disappeared through the archway and soon the sound of the hoof beats were muffled by the snow and faded altogether. Picking up the warm, silky body of the cat and whistling to the dog, which had chased the dog cart to the archway, barking exuberantly, I went back into the house and bolted the front door behind me.

The first thing to do was to explore the house and ascertain where the various books were that I had come to work with, and thus to make up my mind which rooms I needed to open. On a table in the hall I had spotted a large six-branched silver candelabra loaded with candles and with a box of matches lying beside it. I decided to use this in my exploration since it would relieve me of the tedium of having to open and close innumerable shutters. Lighting the candles and accompanied by the eager, bustling dog, whose nails rattled on the bare floors like castanets, I started off.

The whole of the ground floor consisted of three very large rooms and one smaller one, which comprised the drawing-room, the dining-room, a study and then this smaller salon. Strangely enough, this room – which I called the blue salon since it was decorated in various shades of blue and gold – was the only one that was locked, and it took me some time to find the right key for it. This salon formed one end of the house and so it was a long, narrow, shoe-box shape, with large windows at each end.

The door by which one entered was mid-way down one of the longer walls and hanging on the wall opposite was one of the biggest mirrors I have ever seen. It must have been fully nine feet high, stretching from floor level almost to the ceiling and some thirty-five feet in length. The mirror itself was slightly tarnished, which gave it a pleasant blueish tinge, like the waters of a shallow lake, but it still reflected clearly and accurately. The whole was encompassed in a wide and very ornate gold frame, carved to depict various nymphs and satyrs, unicorns, griffons and other fabulous beasts. The frame in itself was a work of art. By seating oneself in one of the comfortable chairs that stood one on each side of the fireplace one could see the whole room reflected in this remarkable mirror and, although the room was somewhat narrow, this gave one a great sense of space.

Owing to the size, the convenience and – I must admit – the novelty of the room, I decided to make it my living-room, and in a very short space of time I had the dust covers off the furniture and a roaring blaze of chestnut roots in the hearth. Then I moved in the cage of finches and canaries and placed them at one end of the room together with Octavius the parrot, who seemed pleased by the change for he shuffled his feathers, cocked his head on one side and whistled a few bars of the Marseillaise. The dog and cat immediately stretched themselves out in front of the blaze and fell into a contented sleep. Thus, deserted by my companions, I took my candelabra and continued my investigation of the house alone.

The next floor I found comprised mainly of bed- and bathrooms, but a whole wing of the house (which formed the hollow square in which the courtyard lay) was one enormous room, the

Long Gallery as Gideon had called it. Down one side of this long, wide room there were very tall windows, and opposite each window was a mirror, similar to the one downstairs, but long and narrow. Between these mirrors stood the bookcases of polished oak and piled on the shelves haphazardly were a myriad of books, some on their sides, some upside down in total confusion. Even a cursory glance was enough to tell me that the library was so muddled that it would take me some considerable time to sort the books into subjects before I could even start to catalogue and value them.

Leaving the Long Gallery shrouded in dust sheets and with the shutters still closed, I went one floor higher. Here there were only attics. In one of them I came upon the gilt frame of a mirror and I shivered, for I presumed that this was the attic in which Gideon's uncle had been found dead. The mirror frame was identical with the one in the blue salon, but on a much smaller scale. Here, again were the satyrs, the unicorns, the griffons and hippogryphs, but in addition was a small area at the top of the frame, carved like a medallion, in which were inscribed the words: *I am your servant. Feed and liberate me. I am you.* It did not seem to make sense. I closed the attic door and, chiding myself for being a coward, locked it securely and in consequence felt much better.

When I made my way downstairs to the blue salon I was greeted with rapture by both dog and cat, as if I had been away on a journey of many days. I realized that they were hungry. Simultaneously I realized that I was hungry too, for the excitement of arriving at the house and exploring it had made me forget to prepare myself any luncheon and it was now past six o'clock in the evening. Accompanied by the eager animals, I made my way down to the kitchen to cook some food for us all. For the dog I stewed some scraps of mutton, and a little chicken for the cat, combined with some boiled rice and potatoes, they were delighted with this menu. For myself I grilled a large steak with an assortment of vegetables and chose from the cellar an excellent bottle of red wine.

When this was ready I carried it up to the blue salon and, pulling my chair up to the fire, made myself comfortable and fell to hungrily. Presently the dog and the cat, replete with food, joined me and spread themselves out in front of the fire. I got up and closed the door once they were settled, for there was a cold draught from the big hall which, with its marble floor, was now as cold as an ice-chest. Finishing my food I lay back contentedly in my chair sipping my wine and watching the blue flames run to and fro over the chestnut roots in the fire. I was relaxed and happy and the wine, rich and heavy, was having a soporific effect upon me. I slept for perhaps an hour. Suddenly, I was fully awake with every nerve tingling, as if someone had shouted my name. I listened, but the only sounds were the soft breathing of the sleeping dog and the contented purr of the cat curled up on the chair opposite me. It was so silent that I could hear the faint bubble and crackle of the chestnut roots in the fire. Feeling sure I must have imagined a sound and yet unaccountably uneasy for no discernible reason, I threw another log on the fire and settled myself back in the chair to doze.

It was then that I glanced across at the mirror opposite me and noticed that, in the reflection, the door to the salon that I had carefully closed was now ajar. Surprised, I twisted round in my chair and looked at the real door, only to find it was securely closed as I had left it. I looked again into the mirror and made sure my eyes – aided by the wine – were not playing me tricks, but sure enough, in the reflection the door appeared to be slightly ajar.

I was sitting there looking at it and wondering what trick of light and reflection could produce the effect of an open door when the door responsible for the reflection was securely closed, when I noticed something that made me sit up, astonished and uneasy. *The door in the reflection was being pushed open still further.* I looked at the real door again and saw that it was still firmly shut. Yet its reflection in the mirror was opening, slowly millimetre by millimetre. I sat there watching it, the hair on the nape of my neck stirring. Suddenly, round the edge of the door, on the carpet, there appeared something that at first glance I thought was some sort of caterpillar. It was long, wrinkled and yellowish-white in colour, and at one end it had a long blackened horn. It humped itself up and scrabbled at the surface of the carpet with its horn in a way that I had seen no caterpillar behave. Then, slowly, it retreated behind the door.

I found that I was sweating. I glanced once more at the real door to assure myself that it was closed because I did not fancy having that caterpillar or whatever it was crawling about the room with me. The door was still shut. I took a draught of wine to steady my nerves, and was annoyed to see that my hand was shaking. I, who had never believed in ghosts, or hauntings, or magic spells or any of that clap-trap, here I was imagining things in a mirror and convincing myself to such an extent they were real, that I was actually afraid.

It was ridiculous, I told myself as I drank the wine. There was some perfectly rational explanation for the whole thing. I sat forward in my chair and gazed at the reflection in the mirror with great intentness. For a long time nothing happened and then the door in the mirror swung open a fraction and the caterpillar appeared again. This time it was joined by another and then, after a pause, yet another.

Suddenly my blood ran cold for I realized what it was. They were not caterpillars but attenuated yellow fingers with long twisted black nails tipping each one like gigantic misshapen rose thorns. The moment I realized this the whole hand came into view, feeling its way feebly along the carpet. The hand was a mere skeleton covered with the pale yellow, parchment-like skin through which the knuckles and joints showed like walnuts. It felt around on the carpet in a blind, groping sort of way, the hand moving from a bony wrist, like the tentacles of some strange sea anemone from the deep sea, one that has

175

become pallid through living in perpetual dark. Then slowly it was withdrawn behind the door. I shuddered for I wondered what sort of body was attached to that horrible hand. I waited for perhaps quarter of an hour, dreading what might suddenly appear from behind the mirror door, but nothing happened.

After a while I became restive. I was still attempting to convince myself that the whole thing was an hallucination brought on by the wine and the heat of the fire without success. For there was the door of the blue salon carefully closed against the draught and the door in the mirror still ajar with apparently something lurking behind it. I wanted to walk over to the mirror and examine it, but did not have the courage. Instead I thought of a plan which, I felt, would show me whether I was imagining things or not. I woke Agrippa the dog and, crumpling up a sheet of the newspaper I had been reading into a ball, threw it down the room so that it landed just by the closed door. In the mirror it lay near the door that was ajar.

Agrippa, more to please me than anything else, for he was very sleepy, bounded after it. Gripping the arms of my chair I watched his reflection in the mirror as he ran towards the door. He reached the ball of newspaper and paused to pick it up. Then something so hideous happened that I could scarcely believe my eyes. The mirror door was pushed open still further and the hand and a long white bony arm shot out. It grabbed the dog in the mirror by the scruff of its neck and pulled it speedily, kicking and struggling, behind the door.

Agrippa had now come back to me, having retrieved the newspaper, but I took no notice of him for my gaze was fixed on the reflection in the mirror. After a few minutes the hand suddenly reappeared. Was it my imagination or did it now seem stronger? At any event, it curved itself round the woodwork of the door and drew it completely shut, leaving on the white paint a series of bloody fingerprints that made me feel sick. The real Agrippa was nosing my leg, the newspaper in his mouth, seeking my approval, while behind the mirror door, God knows what fate had overtaken his reflection.

To say that I was shaken means nothing. I could scarcely believe the evidence of my senses. I sat staring at the mirror for a long time, but nothing further happened. Eventually, and with my skin prickling with fear, I got up and examined the mirror and the door into the salon. Both bore a perfectly ordinary appearance. I wanted very much to open the door to the salon and see if the reflection in the mirror opened as well but, if I must tell the truth, I was too frightened of disturbing whatever it was that lurked behind the mirror door.

I glanced up at the top of the mirror and saw for the first time that it bore the same inscription as the one I had found in the attic: *I am your servant. Feed and liberate me. I am you.* Did this mean the creature behind the door, I wondered? *Feed and liberate me*, was that what I had done by letting the dog go near the door? Was the creature now feasting upon the dog it had caught in the mirror? I shuddered at the thought. I determined that the only thing to do was to get a good night's rest, for I was tired and overwrought. In the morning, I assured myself, I would hit upon a ready explanation for all this mumbo-jumbo.

Picking up the cat and calling the dog (for, if the truth be known, I needed the company of the animals) I left the blue salon. As I was closing the door I was frozen into immobility as I heard a cracked, harsh voice bid me '*Bonne nuit*' in wheedling tones. It was a moment or so before I realized it was Octavius the parrot, and went limp with relief.

Clair the cat drowsed peacefully in my arms, but Agrippa needed some encouraging to accompany me upstairs, for it was obvious that he had never been allowed above the ground floor before. At length, with reluctance that soon turned to excitement at the novelty, he followed me upstairs. The fire in the bedroom had died down, but the atmosphere was still warm. I made my toilet and, without further ado, climbed into bed, with Agrippa lying one side of me and Clair the other. I received much comfort from the feel of their warm bodies but, in addition, I am not ashamed to say that I left the candles burning and the door to the room securely locked.

The following morning when I awoke I was immediately conscious of the silence. Throwing open the shutters I gazed out at a world muffled in snow. It must have been snowing steadily all night, and great drifts had piled up on the rock faces, on the bare trees, along the river bank and piled in a great cushion some seven feet deep along the crest of the bridge that joined the house to the mainland. Every window-sill and every projection of the eaves was a fearsome armoury of icicles, and the window-sills were varnished with a thin layer of ice. The sky was dark grey and lowering so that I could see we were in for yet more snow.

Even if I had wanted to leave the house the roads were already impassable; with another snow fall I would be completely cut off from the outside world. I must say that, thinking back on my experiences of the previous night, this fact made me feel somewhat uneasy. But I chided myself and by the time I had finished dressing I had managed to convince myself that my experience in the blue salon was due to a surfeit of good wine and an over-excited imagination.

Thus comforting myself I went downstairs, picked up Clair in my arms, called Agrippa to heel and, steeling myself, threw open the door of the blue salon and entered. It was as I had left it, the dirty plates and wine bottle near my chair, the chestnut roots in the fire burnt to a delicate grey ash that stirred slightly at the sudden draught from the open door. But it was the only thing in the room that stirred. Everything was in order. Everything was normal. I heaved a sigh of relief. It was not until I was halfway down the room that I glanced at the mirror. I stopped as suddenly as if I had walked into a brick wall and my blood froze, for I could not believe what I was seeing.

Reflected in the mirror was myself, with the cat in my arms, but *there was no dog at my heels, although Agrippa was nosing at my ankles.*

178

For several seconds I stood there thunderstruck unable to believe the evidence of my own senses, gazing first at the dog at my feet and then at the mirror with no reflection of the animal. I, the cat and the rest of the room were reflected with perfect clarity, but there was no reflection of Agrippa. I dropped the cat on the floor (and she remained reflected by the mirror) and picked up Agrippa in my arms. In the mirror I appeared to be carrying an imaginary object in my arms. Hastily I picked up the cat and so, with Clair under one arm and an invisible dog under the other, I left the blue salon and securely locked the door behind me.

Down in the kitchen I was ashamed to find that my hands were shaking. I gave the animals some milk (and the way Agrippa dealt with his left no doubt he was a flesh and blood animal) and made myself some breakfast. As I fried eggs and some heavily smoked ham, my mind was busy with what I had seen in the blue salon. Unless I was mad – and I had never felt saner in my life – I was forced to admit that I had really experienced what I had seen, incredible though it seemed and indeed still seems to me. Although I was terrified at whatever it was that lurked behind the door in the mirror, I was also filled with an overwhelming curiosity, a desire to see whatever creature it was that possessed that gaunt and tallow hand, yellow and emaciated arm.

I determined that that very evening I would attempt to lure the creature out so that I could examine it. I was filled with horror at what I intended to do, but my curiosity was stronger than my fear. I spent the day cataloguing the books in the study and, when darkness fell, once again lit the fire in the salon, cooked myself some supper, carried it and a bottle of wine upstairs, and settled myself by the hearth. This time, however, I had taken the precaution of arming myself with a stout ebony cane. This gave me a certain confidence though what use a cane was going to be against a looking-glass adversary, heaven only knew. As it turned out, arming myself with the stick was the worst thing I could have done and nearly cost me my life.

I ate my food, my eyes fixed on the mirror, the two animals lying asleep at my feet as they had done the night before. I finished my meal and still there was no change to the mirror image of the door. I sat back sipping my wine and watching. After an hour or so the fire was burning low. I got up to put some logs on it, and had just settled myself back in my chair when I saw the handle of the mirror door start to turn very slowly. Millimetre by millimetre, the door was pushed open a foot or so. It was incredible that the opening of a door should be charged with such menace, but the slow furtive way it swung across the carpet was indescribably evil.

Then the hand appeared, again moving very slowly, humping its way across the carpet until the wrist and part of the yellowish forearm was in view. It paused for a moment, lying flaccid on the carpet, then, in a sickening sort of way, started to grope around, as if the creature in control of the hand was blind.

Now it seemed to me was the moment to put my carefully thought-out plan into operation. I had deliberately starved Clair so that she would be hungry; now I woke her up and waved under her nose a piece of meat which I had brought up from the kitchen for this purpose. Her eyes widened and she let out a loud mew of excitement. I waved the meat under her nose until she was frantic to get the morsel and then I threw it down the room so that it landed on the carpet near the firmly closed door of the salon. In the mirror I could see that it had landed near, but not too near the reflection of the hand which was still groping about blindly.

Uttering a loud wail of hunger, Clair sped down the room after it. I had hoped that the cat would be so far away from the door that it would tempt the creature out into the open, but I soon realized that I had thrown the meat too close to the door. As Clair's reflection stopped and the cat bent down to take the meat in her mouth, the hand ceased its blind groping. Shooting out with incredible speed, it seized Clair by the tail and dragged the cat, struggling and twisting, behind the door. As before, after a moment the hand reappeared, curved round the door and slowly drew it shut, leaving bloody fingerprints on the woodwork.

I think what made the whole thing doubly horrible was the contrast between the speed and ferocity with which the hand grabbed its prey, and the slow, furtive way it opened and closed the door. Clair now returned with the meat in her mouth to eat it in comfort by the fire and, like Agrippa, seemed none the worse for now having no reflection. Although I waited up until after midnight the hand did not appear again. I took the animals and went to bed, determined that on the morrow I would work out a plan that would force the thing behind the door to show itself.

By evening on the following day I had finished my preliminary sorting and listing of the books on the ground floor of the house. The next step was to move upstairs to where the bulk of the library was housed in the Long Gallery. I felt somewhat tired that day and so, towards five o'clock, decided to take a turn outside to get some fresh air into my lungs. Alas for my hopes! It had been snowing steadily since my arrival and now the glistening drifts were so high I could not walk through them. The only way out of the central courtyard and across the bridge would have been to dig a path, and this would have been through snow lying in a great crusty blanket some six feet deep. Some of the icicles hanging from the guttering, the window ledges and the gargoyles were four or five feet long and as thick as my arm.

The animals would not accompany me, but I tried walking a few steps into this spacious white world, as silent and as cold as the bottom of a well. The snow squeaked protestingly, like mice, beneath my shoes and I sank in over my knees and soon had to struggle back to the house. The snow was still falling in flakes as big as dandelion clocks, thickening the white piecrusts on the roof ridges and gables. There was that complete silence that snow brings, no sound, no bird song, no whine of wind, just an almost tangible silence, as though the living world had been gagged with a crisp white scarf.

Rubbing my frozen hands I hastened inside, closed the front door and hastened down to the kitchen to prepare my evening meal. While this was cooking I lit the fire in the blue salon once more, and when the food was ready carried it up there as had become my habit, the animals accompanying me. Once again I armed myself with my stout stick and this gave me a small measure of comfort. I ate my food and drank my wine, watching the mirror, but the hand did not put in an appearance. Where was it, I wondered. Did it stalk about and explore a reflection of the house that lay behind the door, a reflection I could not see? Or did it only exist when it became a reflection in the mirror that I looked at? Musing on this I dozed, warmed by the fire, and presently slept deeply, which I had not meant to do. I must have slept for about an hour when I was suddenly shocked awake by the sound of a voice, a thin cracked voice, singing shrilly.

> *'Auprès de ma blonde, auprès de ma blonde,*
> *Qu'il fait bon dormir . . .'*

This was followed by a grating peal of hysterical laughter.

Half asleep as I was, it was a moment before I realized that the singing and laughter came from Octavius. The shock of suddenly hearing a human voice like that was considerable, and my heart was racing. I glanced down the room and saw that the cages containing the canaries and Octavius were still as I had placed them. Then I glanced in the mirror and sat transfixed in my chair. I suffered a revulsion and terror that surpassed anything that I had felt up until then. My wish had been granted and the thing from behind the door had appeared. As I watched it, how fervently I wished to God that I had left well alone, that I had locked the blue salon after the first night and never revisited it.

The creature – I must call it that, for it seemed scarcely human – was small and hump-backed and clad in what I could only believe was a shroud, a yellowish linen garment spotted with gobbets of dirt and mould, torn in places where the fabric had worn thin, pulled over the thing's head and twisted round, like a scarf. At that moment, all that was visible of its face was a tattered fringe of faded orange hair on a heavily lined forehead and two large, pale-yellow eyes that glared with the fierce, impersonal arrogance of a goat. Below them the shroud was twisted round and held in place by one of the thing's pale, black-nailed hands.

It was standing behind the big cage that had contained the canaries. The cage was now twisted and wrenched and disembowelled like a horse in a bull ring, and covered with a cloud of yellow feathers that stuck to the bloodstains on the bars. I noticed that there were a few yellow feathers between the fingers of the creature's hand. As I watched, it moved from the remains of the canary cage to the next table where the parrot cage had been placed. It moved slowly and limped heavily, appearing more to drag one foot after the other than anything else. It reached the cage, in which the reflection of Octavius was weaving from side to side on his perch.

The real bird in the room with me was still singing and cackling with laughter periodically. In the mirror the creature studied the parrot in its cage with its ferocious yellow eyes. Then, suddenly, the thing's hand shot out and the fingers entwined themselves in the bars of the cage and wrenched and twisted them apart.

While both hands were thus occupied the piece of shroud that had been covering the face fell away and revealed the most disgusting face I have ever seen. Most of the features below the eyes appeared to have been eaten away, either by decay or some disease akin to leprosy. Where the nose should have been there were just two black holes with tattered rims. The whole of one cheek was missing and so the upper and lower jaw, with mildewed gums and decaying teeth, were displayed. Trickles of saliva flooded out from the mouth and dripped down into the folds of the shroud. What was left of the lips were serrated with fine wrinkles, so that they looked as though they had been stitched together and the cotton pulled tight.

What made the whole thing even worse, as a macabre spectacle, was that on one of the creature's disgusting fingers it wore a large gold ring in which an opal flashed like flame as its hands moved, twisting the metal of the cage. This refinement on such a corpse-like apparition only served to enhance its repulsive appearance.

Presently it had twisted the wires enough so that there was room for it to put its hands inside the cage. The parrot was still bobbing and weaving on his perch, and the real Octavius was still singing and laughing. The creature grabbed the parrot in the reflection and it flapped and struggled in its hands, while Octavius continued to sing. It dragged the bird from the broken cage, lifted it to its obscene mouth and cracked the parrot's skull as it would a nut. Then, with enjoyment, it started to suck the brains from the shattered skull, feathers and fragments of brain and skull mixing with the saliva that fell from the thing's mouth on to the shroud.

I was filled with such revulsion and yet such rage at the creature's actions that I grasped my stick and leapt to my feet, trembling with anger. I approached the mirror and as I did so, and my reflection appeared, I realized that (in the mirror) I was approaching the thing from behind. I moved forward until, in the reflection, I was close to it and then I raised my stick.

Suddenly the creature's eyes appeared to blaze in its disintegrating face. It stopped its revolting feast and dropped the corpse of the parrot to the ground, at the same time whirling round to face my reflection with such speed that I was taken aback and stood there, staring at it, my stick raised. The creature did not hesitate for a second, but dived forward and fastened its lean and powerful hands round my throat in the reflection.

This sudden attack made my reflection stagger backwards and it dropped the stick. The creature and my reflection fell to the floor behind the table and I could see them both thrashing about together. Horrified I dropped my stick and, running to the mirror, beat futilely against the glass. Presently all movement ceased behind the table. I could not see what was happening but, convinced the creature was dealing with my reflection as it had done with the dog and the cat, I continued to beat upon the mirror's surface.

Presently, from behind the table, the creature rose up unsteadily, panting. It had its back to me. It remained like that for a moment or two; then it bent down and, seizing my reflection body, dragged it slowly through the door. As it did so I could see that the body had had its throat torn out.

Presently the creature reappeared, licking its lips in an anticipatory sort of way. Then it picked up the ebony stick and once more disappeared. It was gone some ten minutes and when it came back it was – to my horror and anger – feasting upon a severed hand, as a man might eat the wing of a chicken. Forgetting all fear I beat on the mirror again. Slowly, as if trying to decide where the noise was coming from, it turned round, its eyes flashing terribly, its face covered with blood that could only be mine.

It saw me and its eyes widened with a ferocious, knowing expression that turned me cold. Slowly it started to approach the mirror, and as it did so I stopped my futile hammering on the glass and backed away, appalled by the menace in the thing's goat-like eyes. Slowly it moved forward, its fierce eyes fixed on me as if stalking me. When it was close to the mirror it put out its hands and touched the glass, *leaving bloody fingerprints and yellow and grey feathers stuck to the glass.* It felt the surface of the mirror delicately as one would test the fragility of ice on a pond, and then bunched its appalling hands into knobbly fists and beat a sudden furious tattoo on the glass like a startling rattle of drums in the silent room. It unbunched its hands and felt the glass again.

The creature stood for a moment watching me, as if it were musing. It was obvious that it could see me and I could only conclude that, although I possessed no reflection on my side of the mirror, I must be visible as a reflection in the mirror that formed part of the looking-glass world that this creature inhabited. Suddenly, as if coming to a decision, it turned and limped off across the room. To my alarm, it disappeared through the door, only to reappear a moment later carrying in its hands the ebony stick that my reflection had been carrying. Terrified, I realized that if I could hear the creature beating on the glass with its hands it must be in some way *solid*. This meant that if it attacked the mirror with the stick the chances were that the glass would shatter and that the creature could then, in some way, get through to me.

As it limped down the room I made up my mind. Neither I nor the animals were going to stay in the blue salon any longer. I ran to where the cat and the dog lay asleep in front of the fire and gathered them up in my arms, then ran down the room and threw them unceremoniously into the hall. As I turned and hurried towards the bird cages the creature reached the mirror, whirled the stick around its head and brought it crashing down. I saw that part of the mirror whiten and star in the way that ice on a pond does when struck with a stone.

I did not wait. I seized the two cages, fled down the room with them, threw them into the hall and followed them. As I grabbed the door and was pulling it shut there came another crash. I saw a large portion of the mirror tinkle down on to the floor and, sticking through the mirror protruding into the blue salon, was the emaciated, twisted arm of the creature brandishing the ebony cane. I did not wait to see more, but slammed the door shut, turned the key in the lock and leant against the

186

solid wood, the sweat running down my face, my heart hammering.

I collected my wits after a moment and made my way down to the kitchen where I poured myself out a stiff brandy. My hand was trembling so much that I could hardly hold the glass. Desperately I marshalled my wits and tried to think. It seemed to me that the mirror, when broken, acted as an *entrance* for the creature into my world. I did not know whether it was just this particular mirror or all mirrors, nor did I know whether – if I broke any mirror that might act as an entrance for the thing – I would be preventing it or aiding it.

I was shaking with fear but I knew that I would have to do something, for it was obvious that the creature would hunt me through the house. I went into the cellar, found myself a short, broad-bladed axe and then, picking up the candelabra, made my way upstairs. The door to the blue salon was securely locked. I steeled myself and went into the study next door where there was, I knew, a medium-sized mirror hanging on the wall. I approached it, the candelabra held high, my axe ready.

It was a curious sensation to stand in front of a mirror and not see yourself. I stood thus for a moment and then started with fright, for there appeared in the mirror, where my reflection should have been, the ghastly face of the creature glaring at me with a mad, lustful look in its eyes. I knew that this was the moment that I would have to test my theory, but even so I hesitated for a second before I smashed the axe head against the glass, saw it splinter and heard the pieces crash to the floor.

I stepped back after I had dealt the blow and stood with my weapon raised, ready to do battle should the creature try to get at me through the mirror, but with the disappearance of the glass it was as if the creature had disappeared as well. I knew my idea was correct: if the mirror was broken from my side it ceased to be an entrance. To save myself, I had to destroy every mirror in the house and do it quickly, before the creature got to them and broke through. Picking up the candelabra, I moved swiftly to the dining-salon where there was a large mirror and reached it just as the creature did. Luckily, I dealt the glass a shivering blow before the thing could break it with the cane that it still carried.

Moving as quickly as I could without quenching the candles I made my way up to the first floor. Here I moved swiftly from bedroom to bedroom, bathroom to bathroom, wreaking havoc. Fear must have lent my feet wings since I arrived at all these mirrors before the creature did and managed to break them without seeing a sign of my adversary. All that was left was the Long Gallery with its ten or so huge mirrors hanging between the tall bookcases. I made my way there as rapidly as I could, walking, for some stupid reason, on tip-toe. When I reached the door I was overcome with terror lest the creature should have reached there before me and broken through and was, even now, waiting for me in the darkness. I put my ear to the door but could hear nothing. Taking a deep breath I threw open the door holding the candelabra high.

Ahead of me lay the Long Gallery in soft velvety darkness as anonymous as a mole's burrow. I stepped inside the door and the candle flames rocked and twisted on the ends of the candles, flapping the shadows like black funeral pennants on the floor and walls. I walked a little way into the room, peering at the far end of the gallery which was too far away to be illuminated by my candles, but it seemed to me that all the mirrors were intact. Hastily I placed the candelabra on a table and turned to the long row of mirrors. At that moment a sudden loud crash and tinkle sent my heart into my mouth. It was a moment or so before I realized, with sick relief, that it was not the sound of a breaking mirror I had heard but the noise of a great icicle that had broken loose from one of the windows and fallen, with a sound like breaking glass, into the courtyard below.

I knew that I had to act swiftly before that shuffling, limping monstrosity reached the Long Gallery and broke through. Taking a grip upon the axe I hurried from mirror to mirror, creating wreckage that a gang of schoolboys would have relished. Again and again I would smash the head of the axe into the smooth surface like a man clearing ice from a lake, and the surface would star and whiten and then slip, the pieces chiming musically as they fell, to crash on the ground. The noise, in that silence, was extraordinarily loud.

I reached the last mirror but one. As my axe head splintered it the one next door cracked and broke and the ebony stick, held in the awful hand, came through. Dropping the axe in my fright I turned and fled, pausing only to snatch up the candelabra. As I slammed the door shut and locked it I caught a glimpse of something white struggling to disentangle itself from the furthest mirror in the Gallery.

I leant against the door, shaking with fright, my heart hammering, listening. Dimly, through the locked door, I could hear faint sounds of tinkling glass; then there was silence. I strained my ears but could hear nothing. Then, against my back, I felt the handle of the door being slowly turned. Cold with fear, I leapt away and, fascinated, watched the handle move round until the creature realized that the door was locked. There came such an appalling scream of frustrated rage, shrill, raw and indescribably evil and menacing that I almost dropped the candelabra in my fright.

I leant against the wall, shaking, wiping the sweat from my face but limp with relief. All the mirrors in the house were broken and the only two rooms that thing had access to were securely locked. For the first time in twenty-four hours I felt safe. Inside the Long Gallery the creature was snuffling round the door like a pig in a trough. Then it gave another blood-curdling scream of frustrated rage and there was silence. I listened for a few minutes but could hear nothing so, taking up my candelabra, started to make my way downstairs.

I paused frequently to listen. I moved slowly so that the tiny scraping noises of my sleeve against my coat would not distract my hearing. I held my breath. All I could hear was my heart, hammering against my ribs like a desperate hand, and the faint rustle and flap of the candle flames as they danced to my movement. Slowly, every sense alert, I made my way down to the lower floor of that gaunt, cold, empty house.

I paused to listen at the bend in the staircase that led down into the hall, and stood so still that even the candle flames stood upright, like a little grove of orange cypress trees. I could hear nothing. I let my breath out slowly in a sigh of relief, rounded the corner and saw the one thing I had forgotten, the tall pier-glass that hung at the foot of the stairs.

In my horror I nearly dropped the candelabra. I gripped it more firmly in my sweating hands. The mirror hung there, innocently on the wall, reflecting nothing more alarming than the flight of steps I was about to descend. All was quiet. I prayed that the thing was still upstairs snuffling around in the wreckage of a dozen broken mirrors. Slowly I started to descend the stairs. Half-way down, I stopped suddenly paralysed with fear, for reflected in the top of the mirror, descending as I was towards the hall, appeared the bare, misshapen feet of the creature.

I felt panic-stricken and did not know what to do. I knew that I should break the mirror before the creature had descended to the level where it could see me, but to do this I would have to throw the candelabra at the mirror to shatter it and this would leave me in the dark. And supposing I missed? To be trapped on the stairs, in the dark, by that monstrous thing was more than I could stand. I hesitated, and hesitated too long, for with surprising speed, the limping creature descended the stairs, using the stick in one hand to support it while the other ghastly hand clasped the banister rail, the opal ring glinting as it moved. Its head and decaying face came into view and it glared through the mirror at me and snarled. Still I could do nothing. I stood rooted to the spot, holding the candles high, unable to move.

It seemed to me more important that I should have light so that I could see what the thing was doing, than that I should use the candelabra to break the mirror. The creature drew back its emaciated arm, lifted the stick high and brought it down. There was a splintering crash, the mirror splinters became opaque, and through the falling glass the creature's arm appeared. More glass fell, until it was all on the floor and the frame was clear. The creature, snuffling and whining eagerly, like a dog that had been shown a plate of food, stepped through the mirror and, its feet scrunching and squeaking, trod on the broken glass. Its blazing eyes fixed upon me, it opened its mouth and uttered a shrill, gargling cry of triumph, the saliva flowed out of the decomposing ruins of its cheeks. I could hear its teeth squeak together as it ground them.

It was such a fearful sight that I was panicked into making a move. Praying that my aim would be sure I raised the heavy candelabra and hurled it down at the creature. For a moment it seemed as though the candelabra hung in mid-air, the flames still on the candles, the creature standing in the wreckage of the mirror, glaring up at me; then the heavy ornate weapon struck it. As the candles went out I heard the soggy thud and the grunt that the creature gave, followed by the sound of the candelabra hitting the marble floor and of a body falling. Then there was darkness and complete silence.

I could not move. I was shaking with fear and at any minute expected to feel those hideous white hands fasten around my throat or round my ankles. Nothing happened. How many minutes I stood there I do not know. At length I heard a faint, gurgling sigh and then there was silence again. I waited, immobile in the darkness and still nothing happened. Taking courage I felt in my pocket for the matches. My hands were shaking so much that I could hardly strike one, but at length I succeeded. The feeble light it threw was not enough for me to discern anything except that the creature lay huddled below the mirror, a hunched heap that looked very dark in the flickering light. It was either unconscious or dead, I thought, and then cursed as the match burnt my hand and I dropped it. I lit another and made my way cautiously down the stairs. Again the match went out before I reached the bottom and I was forced to pause and light another one. I bent over the thing, holding out the match and then recoiled with sudden horror at what I saw.

Lying with his head in a pool of blood was Gideon.

I stared down at his face in the flickering light of the match, my senses reeling. He was dressed as I had last seen him. His astrakhan hat had fallen from his head, and the blood had gushed from his temple where the candelabra had hit him. I felt for his heart-beat and his pulse, but he was dead. His eyes, now lacking the fire of his personality, gazed blankly up at me. I re-lit the candles and then sat on the stairs and tried to work it out. I am still trying to work it out today.

I will spare my readers the details of my subsequent arrest and my trial. All those who read newspapers will remember my humiliation; how they would not believe (particularly as they found the strangled and half-eaten corpses of the dog, the cat and the birds) that after the creature had appeared we had merely become the reflections in its mirror. If I was baffled to find an explanation you may imagine how the police treated the whole affair. The newspapers called me the 'Monster of the Gorge', and were shrill in calling for my blood. The police, dismissing my story of the creature, felt they had enough evidence in the fact that Gideon had left me a large sum of money in his will.

In vain I protested that it was I, at God knows what cost to myself, who had fought my way through the snow to summon help. For the police, disbelievers in witchcraft (as indeed I had been before this), the answer was simple: I had killed my friend for money and then made up this tarradiddle about the creature in the mirror.

The evidence was too strongly against me and the uproar of the Press, fanning the flames of public opinion, sealed my fate. I was a monster and must be punished. So I was sentenced to death, to die beneath the blade of the guillotine. Dawn is not far away, and it is then that I am to die. I have whiled away the time writing down this story in the hope that anyone who reads it might believe me. I have never fancied death by the guillotine: it has always seemed to me to be a most barbarous means of putting a man to death. I am watched, of course, so I cannot cheat what the French, with macabre sense of humour, call 'the widow'. But I have been asked if I have a last request, and they have agreed to let me have a full-length mirror to dress myself for the occasion. I shall be interested to see what will happen.

Here the manuscript ended. Written underneath, in a different hand was the simple statement: *The prisoner was found dead in front of the mirror. Death was due to heart failure. Dr Lepître.*

The thunder outside was still tumultuous and the lightning lit up the room at intervals. I am not ashamed to say I went and hung a towel over the mirror on the dressing table. Then, picking up the bulldog, I got back into bed and snuggled down with him.